Lessons from the Coaches

Lessons from the Coaches

by
R. McKenzie Fisher

New Leaf Press

First printing: May 1997

ISBN: 0-89221-342-6
Library of Congress: 97-65164

Cover by Left Coast Design, Inc., Portland, Oregon

Presented to:

_____

Presented by:

_____

Date:

_____

Dedication

As with all our books, *Lessons from the Coaches* would never have been completed without the love and support of many people. I want to thank:

- **My husband, Ed**, whose love and understanding of uncooked meals and an unkempt house is ever present. Also, thanks for upgrading our computer system and keeping me on-line.
- **Our children, Brian and his new wife, Reneé**, whose love-filled wedding brought even greater joy into my life. (There will be a wedding book someday from all of this.)
- **My dear friends,** (Marsha, Martha, Gene, Erma, and Susan), who coach me along with their encouragement and affirmation.
- **Mary Lee Tracy**, who not only said "Yes" to writing our Foreword but had it back to us in three days!
- **All those mentors** (past and present) who have coached me as well —pastors, teachers, friends, and other authors like Bob and Peggy Benson and Chuck Swindoll. (You'll never know what your letter meant to me!)
- **And to the outstanding coaches Brian had** during his playing days, especially Gary Schulte, Rich Bratten, John Seuberling, and Coaches Kyle and Hollabaugh at DePauw.
- **Last but most important of all, Jesus, who truly is my Life Coach. Without You there would be no lessons of any value**.

Foreword

I hear the question all the time from non-gymnasts, "How do you teach someone to turn those flips and maneuvers on the balance beam?" They say, "I couldn't do that on the floor, let alone on a 4-inch strip of wood four feet off the ground!"

There is a unique reason it's called a BALANCE beam! An athlete needs to be able to balance mental relaxation and physical discipline while performing on this narrow piece of apparatus.

Other types of balance are equally important. Gymnasts, like all athletes, must also balance their diet, exercise, and recovery time. They need to include in their schedule time to study, workout, and have fun with their family and friends.

As I am teaching physical, emotional, and spiritual health to my athletes, I find myself applying the same basic principles to my own life. I have been blessed with some exceptional athletes who balance these factors very well. I think that is one of the reasons our 1996 U.S. Olympic Women's Team selected Amanda Borden as their team captain. She has a real gift of spiritual leadership. We were pleased that NBC's coverage mentioned that she and Jaycie Phelps were partners in Bible study and prayer as well as teammates. (Both Amanda and Jaycie train with us at Cincinnati Gymnastics.)

It has been even more difficult to keep everything in balance after being an assistant coach to the USA team that won the first-ever Olympic Gold Medal in gymnastics. We have many requests for speaking engagements, interviews, and appearances, as well as the need to give back after being blessed with so much success. When Rita approached me to write the foreword for this book, I felt it was one way I could share my faith that could benefit others.

I like the way Rita shares that life lessons can be learned in everything we choose to do. I whole-heartedly agree. It is also nice to see a book where gymnastics is included with other prominent sports of today.

Most of the lessons in this book (and others in the All-Star Series) cross over from one sport to another. What we learn from participating in gymnastics can be helpful in playing any sport. The discipline learned can transfer to all of life's endeavors. Visualization, focus, and teamwork (even in what is often seen as individual sports) are only three of those ideas Rita shares in *Lessons from the Coaches*.

Even though this book is written from a coach's perspective, anyone who enjoys sports can learn a lot from the lessons. Athletes, parents, and fans can find facts, trivia, and inspiration that will apply to many situations both in and out of the sports arena.

Dreams do come true when our goals and desires meet up with God's perfect plan and timing for our life. "I can do all things through Christ who gives me strength" (Phil. 4:13).

In God's Love,
Mary Lee Tracy

Introduction

I haven't dealt much personally with coaches. The only team sport I played was softball and I haven't played that for 20 years. I have watched and assisted several coaches our son Brian played for down through the years. As the official scorekeeper/statistician for nearly all of his summer baseball teams, I worked closely with his coaches.

My husband, Ed, coached Brian for his first few years in Little League — both baseball and basketball. I'm proud of the job Ed did. He taught excellent basics and always played every kid. I'm also proud of the standards he set and the role model he has been, not only for Brian, but also for other young men in our community, some who didn't always have a dad at home.

Of all the coaches Brian had over the years, my favorite (other than Ed, of course) was probably Coach Gary Schulte who coached varsity basketball at Milford High School. He was tough on the guys, but he was fair, set goals, and had some fun along the way. He was an excellent teacher — both on the court and in his math classes. He also had a good rapport with the parents — something many high school coaches lack. He started off calling me "Mrs. Fish," which is where some of the kids picked up the "Mama Fish" tag I carry to this day.

Coach Schulte encouraged the parents to be involved in "spirit" ideas, so we held large banners along highways, cooked spaghetti-pizza dinners (not fund-raisers but for fellowship for the boys), and even sang songs. My favorite event was the night he turned 40 and all the parents wore black.

We even got the announcer (at an away game yet!) to lead "Happy Birthday." I still have a banner with one of Coach Schulte's mottoes: "Can Do!"

I like that! I think I am, by nature, a positive person, so I like people who believe they "can do" anything. When I asked Mary Lee Tracy to write the Foreword for this book, I was thrilled to see the Scripture she chose.

We truly can do anything when God is on our side. The trick is making certain we let Him do the coaching. Too often, I'm afraid I go charging ahead, calling my own plays, and running the game the way I think is best. I'm trying harder to listen for His calls.

I do know that His game plan is far superior to mine. I've seen how He has worked in my life, directing me and connecting me to the right people at just the right time. *His* timing is always perfect! He truly is the greatest coach and role model we have. Let Him guide you as you read this book and through every endeavor in your life.

I hope you enjoy *Lessons from the Coaches*. Like all of the other books in our series, the athletes and coaches in these stories are human beings. I am in no way holding all of them up as Christian role models. Some of them are indeed wonderful Christians, so I may quote them in the latter portion of a lesson. However, we should remember that it is Christ we are to follow.

In Christ,
Rita McKenzie Fisher

Lesson 1
Never Alone

When Jacksonville, in only their second year as an NFL franchise, beat Denver to advance to the AFC Championship game, they did it in the midst of mostly Bronco fans at Mile High Stadium. However, when the Jaguars returned to Jacksonville, they were overwhelmed to find 40,000 fans waiting to enthusiastically greet them in their own stadium at 1:30 a.m.

Only a few weeks later, after winning Super Bowl XXXI, several Green Bay players talked about the importance of fan support. "This trophy belongs to our Packer fans," said QB Brett Favre and others.

While there is often a roar from the spectators sitting near the green when PGA players make their approach, for the most part, golf is a more sedate sport with rather restrained fans. Arnie's Army (Palmer followers) or the new rush of Tiger Woods' fans may be a bit more vocal, but you don't hear the constant yelling from spectators like at football, basketball, or hockey games.

Only the caddie may walk with the player on the golf course. He/she may offer advice, but a player's personal coach is not permitted to make suggestions of any kind. Only between rounds (at the end of 18 holes of play) may a player confer with his/her coach. Imagine a football team playing all four quarters without any signals or plays being sent in by the coaches! "You're basically on your own out there," says British golf star, Nick Faldo, "you can't call your local professional."

Tennis is very similar in that respect. USTA Rule 31 states: "A player may not receive coaching during the playing of any match." During individual or doubles play, this includes no vocal advice, no hand signals, **no** contact. A coach may give suggestions during an "authorized rest period" — when a player leaves the court between sets. This may only occur after the second set in women's play and after the third set in men's matches. In team competition (like Davis Cup), a captain sitting courtside may only offer advice when players change ends of the court at the conclusion of a game. That does not include changing ends during tie-break points. Should a coach be caught trying to give advice even in a discreet or hidden-signal manner, a point can be awarded to the opponent. After a warning, an offending player may be disqualified.

Both golf and tennis are very much individual sports from this perspective. You may receive excellent counsel and instruction in advance, but once the game begins, you really **are** "out there on your own."

Many times in life we feel the same way. We may feel alone even in a crowd if we think no one understands or cares about a problem we are facing. Sometimes we behave in such a manner as to drive others away, leaving us standing (or sitting at home) all alone.

We do not have to be alone, however. During times when others do not seem to understand (sometimes even when they try), there is Someone who will stand beside us — No Matter What! God did not create us to be alone. In fact, He created us so He would not be alone. He desires our companionship and friendship.

If you do not know and feel the friendship of God, take these simple steps to bring Him into your life as a constant companion. Admit that you are human and have sinned. We all have (Rom. 3:23). Understand that Jesus came as God's Son to die on the cross for our sins so that we might be restored in our relationship to God (John 3:16). Ask God to forgive you, and determine to walk each day with Jesus as your example (Acts 3:19–20).

Others may coach you and help you come to an understanding of God's love and grace, but you alone must make the decision. Once you make it, you will never walk alone.

[Jesus talking]: *"And surely I will be with you always, to the very end of the age"* (Matt. 28:20).

"God said that there is only one way to get men back . . . to send Jesus Christ to die for them. He's our way back [to fellowship with God]." — Joe Gibbs (former coach of the 3-time Super Bowl Champion Washington Redskins)

Lesson 2
Golden Shoes
for a Golden Run

Nike would like us to remember the golden shoes they had specially designed for Michael Johnson's run at the 1996 Olympics, but the talented athlete could have apparently run in bare feet and beat the pack. No one came close to this "man in motion." He was a blur on the track even in the early heats.

First edging the Olympic record in the 400-meter race, Johnson's 43.49 was only .2 off the world mark. "The individual gold was more important to me than the world record," he told the press, because he had missed a medal in Barcelona four years earlier when a severe case of food poisoning slowed him down.

Nothing would deter him from winning not one, but two, gold medals in Atlanta. If he "barely missed" the 400-meter record, then he made up for it by shattering his own 200-meter world mark record by .34 of a second. When his time of 19.32 flashed on the clock, even Johnson himself was shocked. "I thought I could do 19.5," he said, "but not this."

Aiming for the Olympic double (200 and 400 gold medals in the same year), Johnson had trained for these games with tremendous intensity. He had rigorously followed the personal training schedule set up by his coach and mentor, Clyde Hart. It was a regime they had been perfecting since Johnson's days at Baylor University. It also included a genuine friendship with Hart as his mentor.

"Of all the experts you surround yourself with, the most important and most rare is your mentor," says Johnson, "the person whose wisdom you draw from in your personal quest."

The entire Johnson family liked Hart's approach right off the starting block. On one recruiting visit, he talked more about the degree Johnson would earn than which events he would run.

"Clyde Hart was the perfect guru," says Johnson, who sees Hart as a "plain-spoken, joke-cracking track coach who knew sprinters the way no one else did." Johnson credits Hart for his training methods and the confidence he instilled.

However, Johnson recognized he had to put forth the effort himself. "A good mentor offers direction and driving tips from the back seat," explains Johnson. "*You* still have to drive the car."

And drive he did! Johnson was a true workhorse. Hart tells of a time when all the other athletes took the day off due to bad weather. He found Johnson out on the track in a "driving rainstorm." When the coach approached him, Johnson grinned and said, "You never know when you might have to run in the rain." Johnson emphatically says that he never missed a scheduled day of training in ten years.

Note, he did say "scheduled"! He didn't say he never took a day off, but when the coach set a schedule that would make Johnson the kind of runner he desired to be, he was willing to follow the plan.

We need to be as intentional in our daily lives. We never know when the storms of life may come. Following a schedule for study, prayer, and worship is the best way to prepare ourselves for any event. Just like the finely trained athlete, we must discipline ourselves to take time for devotions.

Author Richard Foster tells us that the disciplined person is "the one who can do what needs to be done when it needs to be done." That doesn't happen by accident. It takes planned effort. Just like the Olympic athlete, we must train daily. "Discipline works within us as an ingrained habit structure of righteousness, peace and joy in the Holy Spirit," shares Foster, "so that we are free to respond to the situation of the moment in whatever way is appropriate."

What is your spiritual training program? Set up a plan and stick to it!

"The Proverbs of Solomon . . . for acquiring a disciplined and prudent life, doing what is right and just and fair" (Prov. 1:1–3).

"When you are away from the track, it's important to have the same self-discipline. If you are disciplined at home and at work, the habits are reinforced that much more." — Michael Johnson

Lesson 3
Recruiting

After 25 years of coaching at LSU, Dale Brown announced he was stepping down at the end of the 96-97 basketball season. His teams had a successful record: ten seasons with 20 or more wins, four Southeast Conference titles, 13 NCAA appearances including two in the Final Four.

Brown made it clear that he hadn't lost his love of the game. What he had come to deplore was all the nit-picky NCAA rules and the level to which recruiting had climbed. "Recruiting at its present state is absolutely ludicrous," said an almost irate Brown. He felt some summer All-Star camps and AAU programs were out-of-control.

He went on to share perhaps the crux of his displeasure — how some athletes come in "expecting favors, thinking *me* instead of *we* — with a kind of *You-can't-touch-me!* attitude."

Other college coaches share disappointment with the way recruiting has changed. Gene Keady, head coach at Purdue University, doesn't like the limitations placed on coaches by the NCAA in how often you can visit players. "You don't get to evaluate them like you used to," he shared. "You don't get to be around them and see what they're like character-wise, whether or not they'd really take the work ethic we have."

It's hard to get a fair idea if a player might have a problem with drugs or some social issue. High school coaches, looking for the prestige of sending their players to the next level, aren't going to say anything bad. Once a player gets to the university, however, the coach is held accountable for the off-the-court actions of his players.

Basketball broadcaster and guru, and former coach himself, Dick Vitale feels coaches unfairly take the heat for their kids. "If a player is arrested for disorderly conduct, his coach is held under a microscope," says Vitale. "If an English major gets in trouble, the American Lit professor doesn't get blamed. No one even bothers to find out who the teacher is."

Another issue that concerns Vitale is the advantage the larger, more high-profile schools have. Using Michigan as an example, he says the vast number of alumni filled with "Wolverine pride" can influence athletes without anyone so much as buying the kid a bumper sticker. Michigan is also located in a great college town with lots of social life on campus, has a great academic rating, and had the "Fab Five" to draw media coverage to its program. Other schools have similar reputations and trappings as well.

This can cause another headache for coaches at these schools. *Everyone* wants to play for teams like the Kentucky Wildcats, but Rick Pitino only has so many scholarships and so many spots on the bench. Who sits the bench? Once you convince several great players to come to your school, how do you satisfy them all? (At least football coaches have 11 on the field at a time and run separate offensive and defensive squads.) Some athletes, better suited to a smaller or less well-known school, are drawn in by the lure of a potential championship. But, if they sit on the bench, they become disenchanted and either leave the program or give the coach bad press.

We all like to participate. Remember the old schoolyard

games when the two kids got to "choose sides"? First they "took" their best friend. Then they claimed teammates based on athletic ability. But, someone was always chosen last. Was that ever you?

Author and speaker Bob Benson (a frail man even prior to his illness and death) remembered those childhood days well. That's what makes God's love of us so wonderful and unique. We don't have to be big and strong or able to play well — whatever the game in life might be. "Fortunately my being chosen doesn't grow out of me," wrote Benson. He explained God's selection process: "I am just a *choosee*. It was not something in me that made Him call me. It was something in Him. It began in His love for me." Benson continued talking about God's choosing us, "It was not mandatory, deserved, necessary, imperative, or forced. It was His open, voluntary, willful, deliberate, intentional choice. *He chose me*."

God chose 12 ordinary men from various walks of life to be His disciples. Won't you let Him choose you?

[Jesus speaking] *"You did not choose me, but I chose you"* (John 15:16).

"Some high school and junior college players have agents . . . all of these things contribute to making athletes spoiled." — Dale Brown (LSU)

Lesson 4
Doing Your Best

"You need a dream. Set goals. Practice. Concentrate a lot. Work really hard. Put everything into it. Do your best. But above all else, have fun!" That's the message four-time Olympian-turned-coach Jim Terrell not only shares with youngsters but has lived during his athletic career.

Terrell began recreational canoeing with his family when he was 4 years old. At age 6, he placed second in a 14-year-old race. At age 11, watching the 1976 Summer Olympics, he was fascinated with the flatwater canoes. "That's what I want to do," he told his parents.

Eight years later, Terrell fulfilled that dream by qualifying for the Olympic games in Los Angeles. He also raced at the games in Seoul, Korea, in 1988.

Wanting to encourage growth in the sport he loves, Terrell turned athlete/coach after the 1988 games. He became the canoe/kayak director of the Newport Beach (CA) Aquatic Center. After racing in the 1992 Barcelona Olympics, Terrell retired from competition. While he did not win a medal at the Olympic games, he has won 27 Olympic Festival medals, more than anyone in U.S. Olympic sport history. A national champion of his sport for 14 years, Terrell also has 8 Pan Am medals (including two gold) and over 40 national medals.

Back in southern California, he became instrumental in developing a program for at-risk students in the Santa Ana area. Called Project Pride, kids who were discipline and truancy

Jim Terrell
Olympic Canoeing Coach

problems at school were permitted to train free-of-charge if they improved their attendance and grades. Impressed with their accomplishments, Terrell decided to finance a trip to the 1995 Nationals in Indianapolis. They won the Bantam (13 years old and under) category.

Catching the competitive spirit, the kids encouraged Terrell to race again himself. They wanted to see their mentor and friend in the 1996 Olympics. With the games coming to Atlanta (not far from Terrell's own home in Ohio), it was hard to refuse. This time he would be racing not just for himself and his country but as an example for these youngsters. Terrell left the center and began full-time training for his quest. Sweeping every C-1 (single-man canoe) event in the United States, Terrell was undefeated during 1995–96. He qualified for the national team in both the 500-meter and 1000-meter events at the hemispheric trials for the Olympics. He entered only the 500-meter race in Atlanta, allowing another teammate the honor of being an Olympian in the 1000. One of Terrell's regular students, Lia Rousset, also made the Olympic team in the Kayak 2-person 500-meter race.

Terrell made the semi-finals — missing the finals by less than two seconds. He turned in the second best time ever of his career. "I had a good time training and put together the best race I could," says Terrell. "Other guys just had more experience and were stronger, but I am happy with my race and enjoyed my Olympic experience." While taking home a medal would have been glorious, Terrell offered the kids a living example of his coaching (and life) philosophy.

Before moving back to Ohio, Terrell helped coach the youngsters at their national championships. They won the team trophy and every age category except one. Perhaps one of these very students may be the first flatwater canoe sprinter to win an Olympic medal for America someday. Medals or not — canoeing or in other life endeavors — they have learned well the lessons Coach Terrell taught.

The same lessons transcend our daily lives. Setting goals. Working hard. Staying focused. Doing our best. That is all God asks of any of us. Winning isn't His number one goal.

Montreal manager Felipe Alou said, "After the 1994 baseball season, when we didn't get a chance to win [in the play-offs], the Lord seemed to tell me, 'I didn't send you here to win the pennant; I sent you here to be a witness for Me.' Alou assures Expo fans that they will continue the quest for a championship, but he has found a greater purpose in life.

What purpose does God have for your life? Are you setting your goals based on His purpose? Focus on Him. Work hard. Do your best. And, enjoy life along the way.

"Commit to the Lord whatever you do, and your plans will succeed" (Prov. 16:3).

"Not everybody can win. Only one person wins. Try your best and be happy!" — Jim Terrell

Lesson 5
Inspiration

"Win one for the Gipper!" may be one of the most famous lines in college football history. Notre Dame coach Knute Rockne used it to motivate his 1928 team to a 12-6 victory over Army. The Gipper was George Gipp, Fighting Irish kicker and quarterback star who, when dying of pneumonia, told Coach Rockne to someday tell his teammates to win in his memory.

Another football coaching legend, Vince Lombardi of the Green Bay Packers, was renowned for his motivational talks. Coming to Green Bay in 1959 to a team whose most recent record was 1-10-1, the new coach's opening line at his first team meeting was: "If you don't want to play winning football, get out of here right now." They had a winning season in Lombardi's first year, won their division the next season, and the NFL Championship the next. They would also win the first two Super Bowls. Coaches in every sport have used Lombardi's famous line: "Winning isn't everything — it's the only thing!"

Coach of the USA hockey team at the 1980 Lake Placid Olympics, Herb Brooks used a more subdued approach: "You were born to be hockey players," Brooks told the red, white, and blue clad team in the pre-game locker room. "You were meant to be here. The moment is yours."

Even in individual sports like golf, a coach or mentor can offer inspiration. LPGA star Sandra Palmer phoned coach Harvey Penick the day before she won her first U.S. Open. Harvey questioned her, "Are you wishing to win, or do you really have the desire?" Palmer assured him she had the desire. "Then let God's hand rest on your shoulder," said the quiet Penick, "and if it's your turn to win, you will." She did.

Letting God's hand rest on our shoulder should be the comforting motivation in each of our lives — no matter what we do. Where do we turn to get His words of inspiration?

Obviously, the most direct source is the Bible. There is no substitute for reading God's Word. Author and president of Dallas Theological Seminary, Chuck Swindoll says we have benefits over early followers of Jesus. While they had some portions of Scripture, we now have the entire Holy Bible. Swindoll also reminds us that "we can have confidence to approach God" because Christ has also sent the Holy Spirit to be our "Helper." Swindoll translates the Greek words for Holy Spirit — *para* and *kaleo* — to mean "alongside."

Reading other reputable Christian authors like Swindoll is another excellent source of encouragement and inspiration. Paul Meier, John Powell, Chonda Pierce, Luci Swindoll (Chuck's sister), Steve Arterburn, Bill Hybels, Patsy Clairmont, Tony Evans — the list is endless.

"A man finds joy in giving an apt reply — and how good is a timely word!" (Prov. 15:23).

"I can tell the difference in my thoughts and actions on days I skip my quiet times at home — when I don't read the Scriptures, I feel a difference in how I react to different situations." — Fred Goldsmith (Duke University head football coach)

Lesson 6
Coaching for Gold

Most people will recall Bela Karolyi carrying tiny ankle-wrapped Kerri Strug to the gold medal stand for the U.S. Women's Gymnastics team at the 1996 Olympics. His wife, Marta, was the head coach with Mary Lee Tracy as the assistant. Their coaching styles are very different but added a balance to the success of the "Magnificent Seven" (as the U.S. team would be called).

All coaches believe in teaching the basics and commitment to a strict training regime. However, in motivating her students, Tracy has a more quiet, positive, nurturing approach. Regardless of the scoring, she is always there with a hug, a smile, and a gentle word of encouragement.

At the U.S. Nationals, two of Tracy's students, Jaycie Phelps and Amanda Borden, came in second and fourth respectively. Thrilled for both girls, Tracy said, "I want them to remember those feelings because you strive for them again." She also said it was "the highlight of my career" (not realizing she would soon be tapped to help coach the U.S. team in Atlanta).

Karolyi's response at the Nationals: "It wasn't the happiest night of my life." He had been hoping for tiny Dominique Moceanu to be in the media spotlight as his "next Mary Lou" [Retton — former Karolyi gold medalist]. Moceanu came in third, but Karolyi felt disappointed because his pupil wasn't first.

When the final event at the Olympics allowed Strug to

become the heroine in Atlanta, Karolyi gave his attention to her. Although not a 1996 team coach, Karolyi was still on camera, coaching from just outside the restricted area. Hopping on one foot at the end of the vault runway, Strug decided she could go one more time.

"Shake it out!" Karolyi encouraged her. "We gotta go one more time!"

Landing the vault on a badly sprained left ankle, Strug hobbled off the mat, feeling she had done her job for the USA team. Karolyi later said, "She has the satisfaction of knowing she was the one who fulfilled the dreams of six others."

While you can't take away from the courage of Strug, she alone did not "win" the gold medal for the team. The U.S. actually had enough points and moved into first place prior to Strug's final vault. Every other American gymnast had given an outstanding performance to help bring home the first U.S. women's team gold medal in history. Shannon Miller became the most Olympic-medal-decorated female gymnast in U.S. history at the '96 games. Her performances and those of Phelps, Borden, Moceanu, Dominique Dawes, and Amy Chow all counted along with Strug's in the total point count to win the gold medal. It was a true team effort.

Mary Lee Tracy's coaching approach is totally team-oriented. Even though these young women had been competing against each other only one month earlier, Tracy said, "This is the best team effort I've ever seen."

Tracy's pupil, Borden, was elected captain of the '96 Olympic team in large part because of her bubbly-yet-calm demeanor and her spiritual leadership. When Dawes' nerves were causing her stomach to cramp,

Borden told her, "You've got to stay calm and believe in yourself." Sharing a hug with her teammate, Borden offered a final encouragement, "God is there to guide you." Dawes performed one of her best bar routines of the games.

Encouraging one another should be the role of every Christian. Instead, too often individuals seek their own glory or believe their role in the church makes them more important than other members of the congregation.

The apostle Paul writes that in the body of Christ each part has equal importance. "The eye cannot say to the hand, I don't need you!" (1 Cor. 12:21). Paul reminds us, "Just as each of us has one body with many members, and these members do not all have the same function, so in Christ, we who are many form one body, and each member belongs to the other" (Rom. 12:4–5).

Serving Christ together — on His team — is how we reach for true gold!

"Now you are the body of Christ, and each one of you is a part of it" (1 Cor. 12:27).

"We have put our egos aside and have come together as one." — Mary Lee Tracy

Lesson 7
The Coaching Team

Teamwork is blending together into a single unit a variety of individuals often with opposite personalities. That must happen not just among players but within the coaching staff as well.

Normally from three to five assistants can be found on the bench at professional basketball games. NCAA rules limit the number of full-time paid assistants, but some programs add additional staff with part-time and/or volunteer positions. Watching teams like the NBA Raptors or the University of Cincinnati, you might guess one assistant's role is to restrain head coaches like Darrell Walker and Bob Huggins when they get too heated in disagreeing with the referees' calls. In other situations, the roles are reversed. While the head coach meets with the team in the huddle, an assistant will still be harping at the official.

Professional baseball managers usually like to yell at the umpires themselves. Seldom do you see the pitching coach or even the base coaches argue to the point of getting thrown out of the game. Some managers, however, have built their reputations on such antics. Baltimore often needed someone else on the bench when Earl Weaver managed the Orioles. He was ejected 91 times during his career.

During the second year of his managing career in Cincinnati, Ray Knight put together a unique staff. A former Reds player himself, Knight selected other ex-Reds to fill out his coaching roster, including Don Gullett as pitching coach, Tom Hume in the bullpen, Dennis Menke as hitting coach, Ron Oester for infield instruction, and Ken Griffey Sr., to help outfielders. Griffey also coached first base when the Reds were at bat, with Joel Youngblood calling the plays from the third base coaching box. The 1997 Reds are "perhaps the only team in major league history to have a coaching staff made up completely of former players for the team." (*Reds Report*)

Former football stars also return to coach where they played, but it would be difficult to fill out a complete staff in this way due to the number of assistants. Ted Marchibroda chose 14 assistants when he took over the Ravens (the Cleveland Browns team that moved to Baltimore). Jimmy Johnson had the same number when he went to Miami to take over for Dolphin coaching icon Don Shula. Specialties are the name of the football coaching game. Most teams have separate coaches for linebackers, the defensive line, tight ends, quarterbacks, running backs, quality control (one for offense — another for defense), special teams, receivers, the secondary, and strength/conditioning. There are also defensive and offensive coordinators. (These two positions are where most owners look to pluck "rookie" head coaches.) Some head coaches also have an assistant head coach. Check out all the assistants the next time you attend a game. You can try to count them during a broadcast but the cameras probably will not pan wide enough or stay on the respective sideline long enough for you to find them all.

Take a look at your own life. How many "assistants" do you find? Whom can you call on when you need advice? Having a small group of close friends with whom you can discuss problems, prospects, and just everyday challenges is wise. They can offer you a variety of perspectives on nearly any issue. Why not consider as many options as possible before you make a decision? Attending a Sunday school class or Bible study is another way to solicit ideas and input for life's daily issues. Discussion-oriented classes offer you the chance to not only listen to others but share your opinions and ideas about important issues as well. These groups can also hold you accountable in adhering to Christian principles in your decisions.

Put together a coaching staff you can trust. This is one way of assuring the most success in your life.

"For lack of guidance a nation falls, but many advisors make victory sure" (Prov. 11:14).

"I was blessed with some of the greatest players ever assembled on one team. But it was my coaching staff that brought them along and helped to mold them into excellent players." — Sparky Anderson (speaking about Cincinnati's Big Red Machine of the 1970s)

Lesson 8
Color-Blind or Blinded by Color

Take a look at the number of African-American or minority players and white players in professional sports. Compare those numbers to whom you see on the coaching bench, and the discrepancy is apparent. With a total of 87 professional teams in the NBA, NFL, and MLB during the 1995–96 seasons, you barely needed the fingers on both hands to count the number of minority head coaches. During the 1995 Sun Bowl, CBS reported that of 23 colleges with head football vacancies, only one went to a minority.

Yet, the success of those who have forged the way in both the collegiate and professional ranks is impressive. Grambling State University football coach Eddie Robinson's record has the most wins in NCAA Division I-AA. His impressive 405-157-15 is trailed at quite a distance by Roy Kidd of Eastern Kentucky with 266 wins. Robinson had only 7 losing seasons in 56 years as head coach, and his Tiger teams won 17 Southwestern Athletic Conference titles.

Check out our "Winning Coaches" lesson to read about Lenny Wilkens, who is the winningest coach in the NBA. In major league baseball, three Most Valuable Players have gone on to win the Manager-of-the-Year Award. In 1996, Yankee Joe Torre was the third, but two great African-American players, Frank

Robinson and Don Baylor, won the acclaim first. Baylor earned his MVP playing with the Angels and his manager's title coaching the 1995 Rockies. Robinson was the only player in major league history to win the MVP in both leagues while with Cincinnati and Baltimore. He was also with the Orioles in 1989 when he was voted Manager-of-the-Year. Prior to managing in Baltimore, he had the helm in Cleveland and San Francisco.

Earning the NCAA Basketball Coach-of-the-Year Award in 1994 was Nolan Richardson at Arkansas. He had won three similar awards in the Southwest Conference, and many other recognitions, including the Courage Award, the highest honor awarded by the U.S. Basketball Writers. He is the only coach in history to lead teams to a national junior college championship (Western Texas), the NIT title (Tulsa) and the NCAA crown (1994 with Arkansas). As of 1996, Richardson led the Razorbacks to the NCAA tournament 11 of his first 16 years at Arkansas, including three trips to the Final Four. From 1990–1996, his teams won 195 games — more than any other team in the nation.

Another outstanding coach who has fought the battles of prejudice to create a successful basketball program is John Chaney at Temple University. As of the 1996–97 season, Chaney's Owls had appeared in 12 of the last 13 NCAA Tournaments.

Tied for fifth on the all-time list of NCAA appearances (18 through 1995) is Georgetown's John Thompson. He has produced such leading NBA stars as Patrick Ewing, Dikembe Mutumbo, and Alonzo Mourning. Thompson has been instrumental in strengthening the Black Coaches Association that deals with issues of admissions policies, academic standards, and scholarships for minorities. This organization also lobbies the Congressional Black Caucus on race-related issues for the universities.

One can only hope that Congress and the athletic world, along with the general population, will soon put these issues of race behind us. In his 1997 Inaugural Address, President Bill Clinton said, "The challenge of our past remains the challenge of our future: Will we be one nation, one people, with one common destiny — or not? . . . Prejudice and contempt . . . cripple both those who are hated, and of course those who hate. Robbing both of what they might become."

God does not look at the color of our skin or our nationality or gender. He sees only the potential for using the talents He has given us. God intends for each of us to become the best possible person we can and to reach out to others with love and help so they can reach their potential as well.

"Man looks at the outward appearance, but the Lord looks at the heart" (1 Sam. 16:7).

"*Forrest Gump* received thirteen Academy Award nominations . . . *Hoop Dreams* was completely snubbed . . . goes to show that a retarded white guy still has a better chance of success than a couple of hardworking black kids." — February 12 — Bill Maher's *Politically Incorrect 1996 Calendar*

Lesson 9
Endurance

Soccer remains one of the fastest-growing sports in America. More and more youngsters turn out to play on soccer fields and at indoor arenas every year. Having the 1994 World Cup in Chicago didn't hurt the popularity of the sport. Major league soccer drew super crowds in its 1996 premiere season. The All-Star game in July drew 78,000 fans and the LA Galaxy averaged over 30,000 per game, with 69,000 for its opener in the Rose Bowl.

Perhaps nothing thrust soccer into the national spotlight more than the U.S. women's team at the 1996 Olympics. Fans — 76,481 of them — packed Sanford Stadium in Athens, Georgia, for the final game — the most fans ever at a women's competition of any sport in the United States. Goaltender Briana Scurry, Joy Fawcett, Shannon MacMillan, Mia Hamm, Michelle Akers, and their teammates became role models for the next generation of female athletes across the nation.

Solid team play was a key in their victory. Coach Tony DiCicco had worked on team spirit and endurance. A month before Atlanta, the team had gone on a team-bonding encounter that included a wall climb and other trust-building activities.

Perhaps the biggest game for the team at the Olympics was the semifinal match against Norway, who had beaten the U.S. in the 1995 World Cup. Akers tied that game on a penalty kick with MacMillan scoring the winning goal in overtime. What a physically and emotionally draining game! Yet, they came back four days later to beat China 2-1 in the finals. They had indeed endured and had the gold medals to prove it.

Head of the Association of German Soccer Teachers, Gerhard Bauer says endurance is a necessity for effective soccer players. During a regulation game (two 45-minute periods in international play), top players may cover up to nine miles a game. He defines endurance as "the physical and psychological strength to overcome fatigue due to prolonged, intense activities and the ability to recover quickly." Bauer and Germany's medical adviser, Professor Liesen, advise tempo-changing programs that include aerobics and jogging interspersed with one-on-one or two-on-two mini-games of skills. Sprints and periods of relaxation also need to be intermingled with these activities. Stretching prior to and following workouts is also important as is a high-carbohydrate diet.

Michelle Akers has had to re-adjust both her diet and endurance training due to diagnosis of Chronic Fatigue and Immune Dysfunction Syndrome (CFIDS). Akers appeared in a Nike commercial during the Olympics with Emmitt Smith of the Dallas Cowboys. She jokingly taunted him because she would be playing "football" in Atlanta while he sat at home. Heading into the 1996 season, Akers (with 85 goals) was the all-time leading scorer for the U.S. Women's National Team. Four-time All-American at the University of Central Florida and Soccer's Female Athlete-of-the-Year in 1990 and 1991, Akers has also become a national star in the Christian media.

She shares with Fellowship of Christian Athlete huddles and has appeared on the cover of their national magazine as well as *Sports Spectrum* and Athletes in Action publications. Akers tells her story of chronic fatigue and endurance. She also shares other difficulties from the past — the divorce of her parents, a divorce of her own, and 11 knee surgeries. In her new book, *Face to Face with Michelle Akers*, she tells how her faith in Christ helped overcome all of these tragedies and brought peace to her life. Her life is a lesson in endurance.

Endurance, or perseverance, is one of the lessons shared on weekend retreats called the Walk to Emmaus, an interdenominational program (called Cursillo in the Catholic Church). "There are two ways to persevere. First, stay in contact with Christ through prayer, reading the Bible, meditation, and the Sacraments (like communion). Second, stay in contact with other Christians. Share in fellowships that bring about growth, encouragement, accountability, and mutual support."

Endurance comes through Christ and other Christians!

"May the God who gives endurance and encouragement give you a spirit of unity among yourselves as you follow Christ Jesus" (Rom. 15:5).

"Thanks to my relationship with Christ, I can not only get through tough times, but use them to strengthen me." — Michelle Akers

Lesson 10
Coaches behind the Mike

It's a natural jump — coaches-turned-broadcasters. Who knows more or can analyze a game better? Still, for some, being that close to the game is just not satisfactory. They return to the sidelines after a year or two in the TV booth. Former Forty-niners head coach Bill Walsh lasted behind the microphone from 1990–92 before returning to coach at Stanford University. He later went back to San Francisco as an assistant. Jimmy Johnson only took one year off between his coaching days with the Cowboys and then the Dolphins. Mike Ditka, former Chicago Bear player and coach, became a commentator for NBC Sports in 1993 and was a popular figure on the "NFL Live" panel. However, the lure of the field beckoned and he returned to coach the New Orleans Saints for the 1997 season.

Sportscaster Cheryl Miller played and later coached at USC prior to becoming one of the premier basketball hosts for Turner Broadcasting. When the NBA finally agreed to finance a women's professional league, Miller took the head coaching position for the Phoenix WNBA team.

Two top basketball broadcasters who have stayed with the media are Digger Phelps and Dick Vitale. Former coach at Notre Dame, Phelps retired in 1991 but didn't turn straight to broadcasting. He was a special assistant to President George Bush, serving on a drug control board and as an official observer in the 1993 Cambodian elections before working NCAA games for CBS and ESPN.

Vitale has become the guru of college basketball. His, "Way to go, baby!" and other high-strung calls of plays and analysis are a signature no other sportscaster can match.

Former Raider football coach John Madden has turned analysis into an art-form. He was one of the first to successfully use the telestrator to diagram moves on the screen while giving viewers a full explanation of the play. Madden has won ten Emmys while at CBS and Fox.

Former head football coach with the Bengals and Buccaneers, Sam Wyche is one of the new broadcast faces. He is articulate, bright, candid, and quick-witted. He is also an amateur magician, so watch for some slight-of-hand tricks in his repertoire of off-field entertainment.

While trickery is **never** an acceptable part of our Christian lives, there is an element of "magic"— **not** voodoo or mysticism or psychics — but that spiritual sensation when we feel God's presence in our lives without fully being able to understand it. Pastor Steve Hoard says, "We limit God by thinking He thinks like we do." While we may have plans for our lives, if we truly listen to God, He may lead us in another direction. Hoard says that God's dream is not always our dream. We must listen with our hearts open to the Holy Spirit.

Are you listening for His dream for you?

"Many are the plans in a man's heart, but it is the Lord's purpose that prevails" (Prov. 19:21).

"Life to me is about challenges and climbing mountains and that's what I intend to do, try and climb another mountain." — Mike Ditka (on signing as coach with the New Orleans Saints)

Lesson 11
Dreams Do Come True

The Yankees' winning the 1996 World Series captivated the nation. New York held the record for number of appearances (33) and wins (22) in World Series history, taking seven of nine titles in the decade of the fifties. But they had not been in the title match since 1981. Finally, the drought was over.

The real story of patience, endurance, and waiting for dreams to come true, however, was not found in the game itself but in the personality of Yankee manager Joe Torre.

At age 56, Joe Torre had been in the major leagues for 37 years. Voted to nine All-Star teams as a player, he then managed the Mets and Cardinals prior to the Yankees. Torre was in 4,272 games before making it to the Series. No person in baseball history had waited so long.

The team credited Torre for fulfilling the "ultimate baseball dream" for all of them. Shortstop Derek Jeter said, "Joe's the reason, right there. Everyone in here respects Mr. Torre." Pitcher David Cone agreed. "He's been doing it all year." Said Cone, "Joe plays to win. He doesn't go by managing lore or by the supposed book. He does whatever he thinks he has to."

While Torre may not have used baseball lore, his family life during the October Classic was the fairy tale headlining the daily news. One sister, Rae, still lives in Brooklyn in the same house where the family was raised. Another sister, Marguerite is a sister for real — a nun serving an elementary school in Queens. A Torre brother, Rocco, had died of a heart attack earlier in the year. Another brother, Frank, also had a bad heart. In fact, he had been in a New York hospital for ten weeks awaiting a heart transplant. (Frank had played pro ball himself and was a part of the 1957 Milwaukee Braves World Series Championship team.)

Adding suspense to the story line, Frank's new heart arrived between games 5 and 6 of the Series. The 64 year old underwent transplant surgery on the off-day and was awake from the anesthesia in time to watch the final game being broadcast only a few miles from his hospital room.

To cap it all off, Torre would be named AL Co-Manager-of-the-Year. He would win the same award at the ESPY's — over Green Bay Packer Coach Mike Holmgren, Chicago Bulls Coach Phil Jackson, and US Women's Olympic Gold Medal Basketball Coach Tara VanderVeer. The Yankees would also beat out the Packers and Bulls for Team-of-the-Year at the ESPN award show.

What a climax! Torre said, "It's been like an out-of-body experience." The entire family shared the joy, helping everyone to understand that baseball is only a game — that there truly are more important events in life. Still, after the years of strikes and labor disputes, their love of the game and the closeness they shared as a family reminded us why baseball has been called America's game. Baseball was finally back, and we were all glad!

Being glad about life and feeling joy is what God wants for us in our daily lives. He doesn't promise that everything will go our way. That is happiness, not joy. Real joy comes from an inner peace and confidence we get only from trusting in Christ. It comes from an "attitude of gratitude" or thankfulness.

Author and speaker Patsy Clairmont found most people are thankful for faith, family, health, and friends. She adds a fifth: the seasons. Clairmont says that autumn activates her senses, spring renews her heart, and summer soothes her stress. "My spirit celebrates in winter," she says. "The frozen sleep of this season prepares us . . . as death gives way to resurrection." Her gratitude is centered on the "Season Maker." Clairmont defines gratitude as "an upward tilt of the heart."

What direction does your heart tilt?

"Let the peace of Christ rule in your hearts. . . . And be thankful" (Col. 3:15).

"There's no doubt that Joe had a lot of talent in New York. But he had to put it together, make it jell, make it mesh."— Johnny Oates (Texas Rangers and 1996 Co-Manager-of-the-Year with Torre)

Lesson 12
Psych Coach

In addition to calculating yardage and reaching for the appropriate club, Tiger Woods' caddie, Jay Brunza, was along to keep the young golfer on track in more than one way.

Brunza, a sports psychologist and captain in the U.S. navy from San Diego, began working with Woods when he was 13 years old. They worked on mind control and hypnotism techniques to help Tiger stay focused in the midst of pressure. He goes into what they call "an instant zone." And, what a zone! With Brunza carrying the bag, Woods won his first U.S. Junior Amateur at the age of 15, then went on for two more USJGA titles, followed by three U.S. Amateur Opens. No other player has accomplished this many back-to-backs in golf history. Brunza no longer caddies for Woods but remains the Team Tiger psych coach.

Sports psychologists were controversial 20 years ago. "It was somewhere between hot motivational talks, gurus, and some catchy techniques," says Rick McGuire, 48, who has helped form the American track and field psychology program. Working to establish that program for 13 years, McGuire (and a staff of 30 volunteers) earned even more credibility with the success of the U.S. track and field athletes (including decathlon gold medalist, Dan O'Brien) at the 1996 Atlanta games.

Working with promising athletes at the Olympic Training Center in San Diego, McGuire says one of the keys is building relationships of trust between his staff and the athletes and coaches. This includes education, Olympic development, team travel, and personal counseling.

One member of the 1996 U.S. track staff, Jim Reardon, enjoys working with younger athletes. In addition to track athletes, Reardon trains and counsels junior and elite level figure skaters. "We try to provide services when they are younger," says Reardon, "so they can build psychological skills at the same time they are developing physically."

When the competition draws near, there's only so much practice ice time a skater will get. Plus, athletes need to conserve energy for their performances. What do they do with the rest of their rink time?

Like nearly every good sports psychologist, Reardon teaches visualization — closing your eyes and "watching yourself perform the perfect program." He also trains students to see "in your mind's eye" some comfortable, pleasant environment. The technique is then used for relaxation to relieve stress prior to a performance.

It's a matter of learning how to stay focused for all of the preliminary rounds without burning out before the finals. It's also being able to let go of a mistake and move on. "Build on things that go well and let go of things that don't," says Reardon.

"Letting go of the past" is something we all need to learn. Holding onto old mistakes (sins) — our own or others' — is unhealthy. Chapel advisor at Asbury Seminary, David Seamonds tells us that an unforgiving spirit causes resentment. That soon turns to bitterness, and one cannot find joy with a bitter heart. So, for our own health and happiness, we need to forgive.

"We need to give up blaming and learn to assume respon-

44

sibility for our own behavior," says Seamonds. However, he warns, "That doesn't mean we assume responsibility for other people's behavior." We can, however, quit playing the blame game and learn to forgive.

Once we forgive, we leave it up to God. Judgment and punishment (if any) are His responsibility. Seamonds reminds us to be realistic. "Realize forgiveness is a process," he says. "Resentment will not necessarily disappear at once." We may have to "give it up" again and again.

"Bear with each other and forgive whatever grievances you may have against one another. Forgive as the Lord forgave you" (Col. 3:13).

"Those who have become proficient at relaxation and visualization skills can through imagery continue to hone their technical skills without diminishing their physical resources." — Jim Reardon

Lesson 13
Celebrity Coaches

With 74 percent of Americans watching sports on TV at least once a week and 70 percent following sports on a daily basis, it's no surprise that athletes have become the top celebrities in modern America. It also follows that the coaches who lead teams filled with All-American athletes are now stars themselves.

Most college coaches are expected to spend time with alumni at fund raising events. Many of them host their own weekly program on local TV to boost their team's fan support. Popular coaches are often marquee names for local marketing ventures. Some who run top programs are also courted by national advertisers. Look for the Nike and Reebok logos on the shirts and shoes of several college coaching staffs.

Sportscaster Dick Vitale, who left coaching before mega-buck contracts were the norm, says college coaches' salaries go far beyond the physical education department and sports arena. In his book, *Holding Court*, Vitale cites a 15-year deal that Duke basketball coach Mike Krzyzewski has with Nike. In addition to a $1 million signing bonus, the contract is stated to be $375,000 a year plus stock options. Coach K's rival at North Carolina, Dean Smith, has a similar although lesser deal with Nike. Vitale reports that Smith donated his $500,000 signing bonus to charity and splits the annual $300,000 payment with his assistant coaches and the UNC library. Some coaches create foundations that will support ongoing charities beyond their lifetime.

Charitable causes and fan interests take up a lot of celebrity coaches' time. Everyone in Kentucky (and thousands more outside the state) can tell you who Rick Pitino is but most can't recall the governor's name. Pitino receives thousands of Wildcat fan letters, which he tries to answer as best he can. In an interview with *Up Close* host Roy Firestone, Pitino told about a man whose wife wanted a divorce. The man was certain his wife would stay in the marriage if Pitino would intervene on his behalf. Pitino passed the letter along to a priest for his reply and counsel.

When Firestone asked the UK celebrity how he keeps his perspective amidst this hero worship, Pitino responded that he had given up on ego. "I'm very happy today because I lost 'I' and 'my' quite a while ago," shared Pitino. He did say he recalled a time when he was more egotistical but was very disappointed with himself in that era.

You don't have to be in the national media to get caught up in the "I" spotlight. Any of us can misuse our finances (and time) to seek personal fame and gratification. It isn't the amount of a contract that is meaningful but how the individual uses those resources. The Bible doesn't say money is the root of all evil but the "love of money." It's also not about how much someone gives. Mark writes in his Gospel about a poor widow whose two mites (equal to 1/2 a penny) were used as the example of pure giving because she was giving all she had. She was giving from her heart.

President Clinton called on former Presidents George Bush, Gerald Ford, and Jimmy Carter, along with former First Ladies Nancy Reagan and Lady Bird Johnson, to lead a summit that would encourage all

Americans to give of themselves. Bush began the "Points of Light" Foundation during his administration, when he recognized individual volunteer efforts as examples of true All-American celebrity. Celebrities are those persons who are famous and held in public esteem. Who better to esteem than those who give of themselves for others?!

What are you giving?

"A good name is more valuable than great riches; to be esteemed is better than silver or gold" (Prov. 22:1).

"These guys [college coaches] are like CEO's of large corporations with the kind of dollars they're generating — the TV revenue, the tournament dollars, the marketing, the T-shirts, the alumni donations." — Dick Vitale

Lesson 14
Heisman Coach

Elite athletes produce other elite athletes in nearly every sport. A list of some of the U.S. Olympic 1996 Coaches-of-the-Year proves that point. Tom Gullickson (a pro in both singles and mixed doubles with his twin Tim for several years) coached the Olympic men's tennis team in Atlanta. He has also coached the U.S. Davis Cup team. Carol Heiss Jenkins (gold medalist, 1960) and Peter Oppegard (bronze medalist) were named top figure skating coaches. Divorced husband of Great Britain's Princess Anne, Capt. Mark Phillips is a former Olympian-turned-coach for the U.S. equestrian team.

Look in any college or professional team media guide and read the background of the coaching staff. It's not unusual to find former NCAA All-American players as successful head coaches. Nowhere was that more evident in 1996 than at the University of Florida.

Head football coach Steve Spurrier won the Heisman Trophy for the top collegiate football player of the year in 1987 while at Duke University. At the conclusion of the 1996 season, Spurrier's quarterback at Florida, Danny Wuerffel, won the award — making this the first time in history a Heisman winner has been coached by a Heisman winner. It was icing on the cake for the two who shared the Number One ranking after beating nemesis-and-rival Florida State in the Sugar Bowl.

Spurrier says he actually enjoys coaching more than he did playing.

Bobby Bowden
Florida State University

"It's fun," he shares, "not like going to work." Long-time friend but rival coach at Florida State, Bobby Bowden agrees but says their approach is totally different. "Steve works out of confidence. I work out of fear." Spurrier states it another way. He says, "Bobby is New Testament. I'm more an eye-for-an-eye like the Old Testament."

Using scriptural references is nothing new to either coach. It is not unusual to hear Bowden speaking as a guest in church pulpits. He shares how he has seen God's plan unfold in his own life. He turned down coaching jobs at Marshall and LSU. In both cases, plane crashes killed those head coaches (and the entire Marshall football team.) Bowden tells others how he has felt God's presence in his life.

Gator quarterback Danny Wuerffel feels Christ's presence as well. Investigating the clean-living quarterback early in the season, one journalist proclaimed, "Interrogating Wuerffel's coaches, teammates, and friends, the reporters found nothing but more squeak in his clean." He doesn't swear, smoke, drink, carouse, use drugs, or cut class. His overall 3.75 GPA earned him recognition as the 1996 National Foundation and College Hall of Fame Scholar-Athlete.

Wuerffel refers to himself with another hyphenated description as a Christian-athlete. He says, "That's a Christian who happens to be an athlete and not visa versa."

Wuerffel isn't ashamed of his moral convictions and his personal relationship with Christ. He attended regular Bible study and wasn't embarrassed for others to know he kneels each night to pray before going to bed. As a member of Florida's Fellowship of Christian Athletes, he also attended rallies for high school students and prayed with his teammates before and after the games. After the Gator game against Tennessee, Wuerffel and Volunteer star Peyton Manning led a large contingent of players from both teams in a mid-field prayer.

Wuerffel is indeed a Christian-athlete. Where do you stand? Are you a Christian-businessman? A Christian-mother? A Christian-student? Where is your emphasis?

"And whatever you do, whether in word or deed, do it all in the name of the Lord Jesus, giving thanks to God the Father through him" (Col. 3:17).

"While the act of appearing righteous to garner public approval is abhorrent to Jesus, it was never His intention to force His children to hide their faith." — Danny Wuerffel

Lesson 15
Vote of Confidence

Without a vote of confidence from their respective coaches, two of 1996's top athletes could have been lost from the world of sports. Ironically, back-to-back articles in *Sports Illustrated (5/27/96)* dealt with the substance abuse of the year's Super Bowl Champ, Brett Favre, and World Series winner Dwight (Doc) Gooden.

While undergoing knee surgery in February of '96, Favre suddenly went into seizures that rendered him unconscious. The complication was caused by his combining prescription painkillers and alcohol. While at Green Bay, former quarterback coach Steve Mariucci had warned Favre and others that continual use of painkillers for injuries should be carefully monitored. Then Mariucci left to coach Cal Berkeley (and later the San Francisco 49ers in 1997). Certain teammates continued to confront Favre, along with girlfriend (now wife) Deanna, who even threatened to take their young daughter and leave.

Favre finally admitted he had an addiction he could no longer handle on his own and checked himself into the Menninger Clinic. Released in time for pre-season training, Favre had the full support of Packer coach Mike Holmgren. While the two had clashed in their beginning at Green Bay, Mariucci (friend to Favre and disciple of Holmgren) may have helped bridge the gap in their relationship. Once Favre felt he had Holmgren's vote of confidence, he went on to become one of the premier quarterbacks in the NFL, winning the 1996-97 Most Valuable Player Award.

Gooden understands what a vote of confidence from a coach (and team) can mean as well. Once the pitching prodigy of the New York Mets, Gooden won the Cy Young Award in 1985 and led his team to the 1986 World Series title. Like Favre, he had a problem with alcohol, but unlike Favre's prescription drug problems, Gooden used cocaine. The world of narcotics literally "drug" him down. After repeated violations of baseball's substance-abuse policies, Gooden was suspended. He, too, went through a successful re-hab program, but in 1995 his only involvement in baseball was coaching a Little League team in Florida. Then, Yankee owner George Steinbrenner called to see if Doc might be interested in a comeback. Yankee manager Joe Torre was supportive of the acquisition, and on May 14, 1996, Gooden became the first Yankee right-hander in 40 years to pitch a no-hitter.

Irony at its best, but it seldom happens that way. Substance abuse (drugs and/or alcohol) is *not* the precursor to success! Not every abuser comes back at all, let alone to climb to the top of his profession. Instead, thousands of lives are ruined each year because of such abuse.

One former professional football coach has spent years trying to counter that problem. When he left as head coach of the Dallas Cowboys after 28 seasons, Tom Landry's record (including two Super Bowl championships) was 270-178-6. Statistics of how many young people's lives he has changed due to his involvement with *One Way 2 Play — Drug Free* are most likely more impressive but cannot be tallied. Landry attends innumerable fund raisers, banquets, camps, rallies, and huddles for the program.

One Way 2 Play is the drug and alcohol program for teenagers and college students sponsored by Fellowship of Christian Athletes. From rallies and assemblies in schools to special events like breakfasts prior to All-Star games (high school through the pro ranks), FCA has found success in being a Christian support group that helps students hold one another accountable. They encourage young people to sign commitment cards that they will refrain from all substance activity. Support groups, known as "huddles," also meet regularly for Bible study and prayer.

Books (with sections by Landry and professional athletes like Brent Jones, David Robinson, Betsy King, and others), bumper stickers, T-shirts and other popular items sport the program's colorful logo and motto:

"No Shootin' — No Slammin' — No Pushin' — No Poppin' —
No Smokin' — No Snortin' — No Boozin' — No Droppin' . . .
CUZ THERE'S ONLY ONE WAY 2 PLAY — DRUG FREE!"

"Wine is a mocker and beer a brawler; whoever is led astray by them is not wise" (Prov. 20:1).

"Student athletes often don't realize the seriousness of drug and alcohol abuse. The consequences can be severe. In fact, it's one of the most difficult challenges young people face today." — Bart Starr (former QB and head coach for the Green Bay Packers)

Lesson 16
Cradle of Coaches

If you happen to be a graduate of Miami (Ohio) University, you will recognize the above title. Otherwise, you probably don't realize that eight national football "College Coach-of-the-Year" Awards have been presented to Miami graduates or those who had their coaching careers begin on the Oxford campus. After leading Army to three consecutive undefeated seasons (1944–46), Earl H. (Red) Blaik won the award in 1946. He also coached back-to-back Heisman Trophy winners in Glenn Davis and Felix (Doc) Blanchard. Woody Hayes, who coached Ohio State for 28 seasons, led the Buckeyes to 13 Big Ten Championships and eight Rose Bowl appearances, winning four of the New Year's Day games. He also developed 58 All-American players and won the coaching award in 1957. Also winning 13 Big Ten titles, but while coaching at rival Michigan, Bo Schembechler won the award in 1969. Other Miamians selected Coach-of-the-Year were Paul Dietzel (LSU 1958), Ara Parseghian (Notre Dame 1964), John Pont (Indiana 1967), Jim Root (New Hampshire 1967), and Bill Narduzzi (Youngstown State 1979).

Professional football teams have also been led by former Miami players and coaches. Wilbur "Weeb" Ewbank coached the NY Jets and before that the Super Bowl Champion Baltimore Colts. Football legend Paul Brown first coached at Miami (then Ohio State) before starting and coaching both the Cleveland Browns and the Cincinnati Bengals. Other Miami graduates in professional football are Bill Arnsparger (assistant coach of San Diego Chargers), Jerry Angelo (director of player personnel with Tampa Bay), and John McVay (general manager of the San Francisco 49ers).

Coaches in other sports who have not only earned their education degree but learned the basics of athletics at Miami are Walter (Smokey) Alston (former Brooklyn and LA Dodger manager), John Shoemaker (LA Dodger minor league coach at Vero Beach), Randy Ayers (former Ohio State head basketball coach), and Wayne Embry (general manager of the Cleveland Cavaliers).

What is it about the training at Miami that instilled such successful traits to earn it the nickname "Cradle of Coaches"? Perhaps it is not a coincidence that Miami is also well-known for its education department. Teachers and administrators with degrees from Miami fill classrooms at every level around the nation. Many of the teaching courses they attended were held in McGuffey Hall, named after William Holmes McGuffey, author of the famed *Eclectic Reader*. More than 120 million copies of *McGuffey's Reader* were used by nearly every American student in first through sixth grades in the 1800s. McGuffey taught at Miami from 1826 to 1836 and became president of rival school Ohio University in 1839. A teacher and clergyman, he included moral values as well as basic knowledge in his books.

Another book that has outsold McGuffey's (and all others throughout history), the Holy Bible teaches us not just knowledge but wisdom as well. Wisdom is the ability to discern and use knowledge correctly. That should be our goal in reading the Bible — to gain wisdom, not to prove history or whether some church doctrine is better than another. Reading God's Word goes beyond arguing whether each parable and story are to be taken literally.

Missionary in Sri Lanka, Ajith Fernando, suggests four questions that will help us glean wisdom and true meaning from our Bible study: "Is there a promise for me to claim? Is there a command for me to obey? Is there a sin for me to avoid? Is there an example for me to follow?" The answers to these questions will teach us how to live each day wisely.

"Let the word of Christ dwell in you richly as you teach and admonish one another with all wisdom" (Col. 3:16).

"The goal is to do the best job you can every year that you coach." — Ara Parseghian (former coach at Miami (Ohio), Northwestern, and Notre Dame)

Lesson 17
Coaching the Tiger

How do you coach a golfer who everyone, including Jack Nicklaus, says already has the perfect swing? Golf pro from Lochinvar Golf Club in Houston, Butch Harmon, has that role with PGA phenom Tiger Woods.

Woods won the junior world championship (for ages 10 and under) at age 8 and collected five different age-group world titles by age 14. (Read the chapter "Psych Coach" for more information about Woods' amateur accomplishments.)

Stanford golf coach Wally Goodwin first wrote Tiger at age 13 and was thrilled when the youngster later chose to attend the university. "He's the best junior player who's ever lived," said Goodwin, "but he's a great kid. He seems motivated to help us attain **our** goal of a national championship." Indeed, Stanford won NCAA titles while Tiger played with them.

The Woods family was determined that Tiger would finish his degree before turning pro, but having reached every pinnacle available to an amateur, he left college for the PGA in the fall of 1996.

Butch Harmon began coaching Woods back in high school. They met in person only twice the first year. Tiger sent monthly tapes to Houston, and they talked every week. With Tiger now on the pro tour, Harmon spends more time traveling as well. He was present when Tiger made the cut in his first ever match as a pro with an opening round of 67 at the Milwaukee Open. Tiger won two of the his first seven PGA events and ended up 24th on the leaders' board for 1996. While he had fully expected

Tiger to play well enough to make the top 125 (earning his playing card for 1997), Harmon said this was the "icing on the cake."

Still, Woods has the desire to improve. One wonders, "At what?" After playing the '96 British Open (as an amateur) with the likes of Greg Norman, Fred Couples, and Nick Faldo, Woods questioned, "Butch, how far away am I? When will I be that good?"

"You just have to keep working," said Harmon, "you've got so much to learn."

Woods played only 41 rounds as a pro on the 1996 PGA tour. It takes 50 to qualify for top awards. However, Tiger made 13 eagles, only three behind leader Kelly Gibson (with 101 rounds). On par-5 holes, Tiger shot either an eagle or birdie 51.5 percent of the time, while Greg Norman won the category with 45.1 percent. Recognized as the longest driver off the tee, John Daly averaged 289 yards. Tiger's average was 302.8 yards. Yet, amazingly he doesn't "give it everything." Harmon coaches him to use "no more than 80 percent effort on most tee shots." The coach believes that level of force keeps his timing and swing more in balance and promotes better accuracy. As good as Woods is, Harmon sees him getting better. They are working on the short game and other intricacies of the game to push him that direction.

Sometimes when we seek God's direction for our lives, He may deal in small changes as well. When we first come to accept His love and forgiveness, we may want desperately to serve Him. However, God does not call all of us into the ordained ministry. Rather than giving up our present jobs and making huge changes in our lives, His call may be for us to share His love with those in our circle of

Butch Harmon
A "Tiger" of a Golf Coach

friends or at work where we are.

Pastor Fred Shaw reminds us that only one percent of people are brought into churches because of the pastor. Eighty percent come because of family and friends. Others show up because "the church is pretty" or "it's next to the high school" or because they are facing a personal crisis.

We may not need to make huge changes in our surroundings to make a tremendous change for Christ in the lives of others. What small thing might you do or say that will help someone follow Christ's direction for their life?

"Let your light shine before men, that they may see your good deeds and praise your Father in heaven" (Matt. 5:16).

"I knew he [Tiger] was the real deal, the bad news is that he has to live up to it." — Butch Harmon

Lesson 18
Winning Coaches

One of the premier divisions of Little League baseball is named for Cornelius McGillicuddy, who changed his name to Connie Mack. He had more wins than any manager in major league history. After managing 53 years, his record of 3,755-3,967 was obviously for most wins, not highest percentage. John McGraw trails Mack in number of wins with a 2,810-1,987 record, and Sparky Anderson is third with 2,238-1,855. Anderson is the only manager to win over 100 games in both leagues and win a World Series in both (Reds in 1975-76 and Tigers in 1984). The remaining top ten winningest baseball coaches are Bucky Harris, Joe McCarthy, Walter Alston, Leo Durocher, Casey Stengel, Gene Mauch, and Bill McKechnie.

Stengel heads the list in World Series wins — managing the Yankees during their legendary run in the 1950s. In 12 years, they won ten American League Pennants and seven World Series. Leaving the Yankees after the 1960 season, Stengel came back to New York two years later to manage the National League Mets. The team lost 120 games that year, but over a million fans came out to see their beloved Casey.

One NBA coach who comes close to Stengel in adoration from the fans and in leading a legendary team is Red Auerbach, former coach and general manager of the Boston Celtics. While coaching, his teams won nine NBA titles, including eight in a row from 1958-59 through 1965-66. When he left the coach's bench, he had the most all-time wins with 938.

Lenny Wilkens passed that mark in January of 1995. He led Seattle to the 1979 NBA title and coached in Portland and Cleveland before coaching the Atlanta Hawks. Wilkens also coached the 1996 Dream Team to their Olympic gold medal. In March of '96, Wilkens became the first NBA coach to reach 1,000 wins.

Detroit Redwing coach Scotty Bowman became the first National Hockey League coach to accomplish the same feat, collecting 1,000 victories on February 8, 1997. He has led teams to six Stanley Cup titles, five with Montreal and one in Pittsburgh. No other NHL coach comes near his record. Billy Reay led teams to 542 victories followed by Toe Blake with 500.

One can't talk about winning coaches without mentioning the great Vince Lombardi. Among other accomplishments, his Green Bay Packers won Super Bowls I & II. (See the chapter "Inspiration" for more.)

Super Bowl III would see the New York Jets beat the Baltimore Colts 16–7. Colts' head coach Don Shula, the youngest in the NFL at that time, would lead Baltimore to a 71-23-4 record before moving on to Miami. He led the Dolphins to two consecutive Super Bowl titles in 1972–73. His 1972 team had the only undefeated season (17-0) in NFL history. When Shula retired from coaching the Dolphins, he had the most wins (347) of any head coach in NFL history. (Former Chicago Bear's coach George Halas is second all-time with 324.)

Shula was replaced by Jimmy Johnson for the 1996–97 season. Johnson had replaced another NFL coaching icon earlier in his career, taking over for Dallas Cowboy Coach Tom Landry in 1989. Named the Dallas coach when they entered the NFL in

1960, Landry had been the only coach Cowboy fans knew. He compiled a 250-162-6 record that included five trips to the Super Bowl, winning two. Johnson also led the Cowboys in winning two Lombardi trophies before being replaced by Barry Switzer. Johnson would turn broadcaster for a year before taking over for Shula in Miami.

One of Shula's favorite sayings is: "Success is not forever, and failure isn't fatal!" NBA Chaplain for the Washington Bullets, Joel Freeman applies that lesson to our victory as Christians. "Regardless of what happens in the future, we can boldly live in a victorious frame of mind," says Freeman. "Christ has made us more than conquerors . . . which means . . . we never have to entertain fear about the future." He explains a favorite scripture, "A conqueror has the victory march *after* he has won the battle, but a more-than-conqueror has the victory celebration *before* he goes to war."

"No, in all these things we are more than conquerors through him [Christ Jesus] who loved us" (Rom. 8:37)

"If your highest authority is . . . yourself or your last victory, you won't be a very effective coach. But belief in something bigger than you is important. It makes a real difference to me when I start off each day by giving thanks and asking for help from God." — Don Shula

Lesson 19
The Wizard

"[Vince] Lombardi was a legend, along with coaches such as Red Auerbach, Casey Stengel, and Knute Rockne," says sports guru Dick Vitale, "but nobody has accomplished what John Wooden achieved at UCLA."

In 40 years coaching basketball, Wooden won over 81 percent of his games with a lifetime record of 885-203. He is the only person (to date) to make the National Basketball Hall of Fame as both a player (1960) and coach (1972). He lettered in both basketball and baseball as a freshman at Purdue University and was voted All-American as a guard for the Boilermaker hoop team for three years. He was captain of the team for two seasons, leading them to two Big Ten titles and the 1932 NCAA Championship.

An English major, Wooden was also an honor student. He taught high school English for 11 years while coaching basketball, baseball, and tennis. His prep record was 218-42. He also coached at Indiana State University for two seasons with a 47-14 record.

At UCLA for 27 years, Wooden set records no Bruin coach may ever match. His final record was 620-147 with a home court advantage at Pauley Pavilion of 149-2. He is the only NCAA coach to lead four teams in a row to undefeated seasons. That's 88 victories in a row! His Bruin teams claimed 10 NCAA titles with 38 consecutive

Coach Wooden
Legendary UCLA Coach

tournament wins. Vitale says, "His accomplishments raised the standard to an unreasonable level."

Wooden has been recognized in nearly every manner possible: Coach-of-the-Year (6 times), Man-of-the-Year (by both *Sporting News* and *Sports Illustrated*), Coach-of-the-Century (Friars Club), several basketball Halls of Fame, and too many other annual or special awards to list. He was the first recipient of the James Naismith Peach Basket Award for Outstanding Contributions to Basketball.

Outside the sporting arena, Wooden was equally honored — receiving the Father-of-the Year award at least twice in California, the Landry Medal for Inspiration to American Youth, the Reagan Distinguished American Award, and the Lexington Theological Seminary Service-to-Mankind Award. He also won awards for his spiritual leadership: the Bellermine Award of Excellence (also given to Mother Theresa) and "Outstanding Basketball Coach in the United States" from his own denomination (the Christian Church).

In his book, *They Call Me Coach*, Wooden shares what he calls the "Pyramid for Success." He talks a lot about being loyal to yourself and to others, especially those who depend on you. He also encourages friendship, cooperation, and team spirit with co-workers on every level. Having reliability, integrity, honesty, and sincerity are high on Wooden's list of necessary characteristics for success as well. Space doesn't permit listing all of the traits that he challenges those around him to absorb into their daily lives, but he puts two powerful ones at the top of the pyramid: faith and patience.

Minister and author Lloyd John Ogilvie, says, "Faith is a

primary gift of the Holy Spirit . . . by which we respond to what God has done for us in Jesus Christ . . . our trust that Christ will follow through in all of life's changes and challenges." Faith is knowing God and accepting who He is. Wooden says this comes about through prayer.

Prayer is simply talking with God. Often listening for God's direction involves the other trait at the top of Wooden's pyramid — patience. Ogilvie says, "Patience is really faith in action. Patience must be rooted in the overarching confidence that there is Someone in control of this universe, our world, our life."

Waiting for God's direction is not always easy. Stated simply, Wooden says: "Good things take time."

"We do not want you to become lazy, but to imitate those who through faith and patience inherit what has been promised" (Heb. 6:12).

"Pray for guidance, count and give thanks for your blessings each day." — #7 on a handwritten note given to John Wooden by his father

Lesson 20
One Coach Overall

Rome: 1960. Eighty-three countries came to Italy for the Summer Olympics with 5,348 athletes vying for gold medals in 150 events. What are the odds of two best friends competing against one another to win Olympic gold and silver medals while representing two different countries? That's exactly what happened.

Rafer Johnson of the United States and C.K. Yang from Taiwan competed in the 1960 decathlon. The ten-event competition was so close that Johnson was ahead by only eight seconds going into the final event — the 1500-meter race. Yang outpaced Johnson to win the 1500 but only by two seconds. Imagine! After ten grueling events, the gold and silver medalists were separated by only six seconds!

Johnson ran to Yang after the race and the two clung to one another. "As good as I felt, I knew he had to be disappointed," said Johnson, "so I had to be next to him."

What had developed this bond and closeness? The two had been track teammates at UCLA and had trained side by side in all of the decathlon events. What makes their story even more poignant is that they shared the same coach. "Ducky" Drake not only had been their Bruin coach but went with **both** of them to the Olympics. Johnson recalls the advice Drake gave each athlete prior to that 1500-meter race. He told Johnson to prepare for a tremendous finish, then walked over to Yang and encouraged him to open a gap in the final 1/4 mile. No one could have been prouder at the medal presentation. Drake had not played favorites but had encouraged each to push the other to higher levels of competition.

Just as Drake was one coach over both athletes, God is one God over all! He loves each of us as individuals. He wants the best for all of us, and He coaches each of us to do our personal best.

Perhaps we come to understand that "love divided is not less love" when we become parents. After loving their firstborn so intensely, many young couples fear that they will not have enough love to share when the next child is born. That fear is soon put to rest when the second infant is placed in its mother's (or dad's) waiting arms. Perhaps, that is one of the best ways we can understand our being made in God's image. Just as we can love each of our children as if he/she were the best, God loves us completely and individually.

Author and storyteller Bob Benson once shared a story about how we limit God. "It's almost like we put him in a box and keep him down at the front of the church," said Benson. He goes on to share that the problem with that concept is that "the box is too small." We limit God by our own limited understanding. God is a greater God than any of us can imagine. He can truly love each of us as if we were the only person in His life. He is indeed One God Over All!

"As iron sharpens iron, so one man sharpens another" (Prov. 27:17).

"Whenever we competed, I never wanted to see C.K. do poorly in anything. I was a better athlete in my total package with C.K. than I would have been without him." — Rafer Johnson

Lesson 21
Substitutes

Fifteen players, mostly college all-stars and several conference MVPs, sit in the locker room. How do you choose which five guys will start the game? How do you keep everyone with the big bucks, and often big egos, happy? Ask NBA coaches Phil Jackson, Pat Riley, or Brian Hill.

It's the same problem in major league baseball clubhouses. No one wants to be a "role player" and come in at the end of the game (except maybe the closing pitchers who have multi-million dollar contracts). No one volunteers to be the back-up quarterback in the NFL either. Steve Young didn't *enjoy* playing second fiddle to Joe Montana, and when Young took over at Number One, Montana left for the playing pastures of Kansas City.

College and high school coaches don't have it any easier pleasing players. Even Little League coaches are bombarded by tiny tikes and their over-zealous parents who think "my kid should be playing more!"

What's a coach to do? Being able to effectively use substitutes off the bench is an important aspect of coaching. "If you happen to make the perfect call, it's a miracle." That's how former Dodger manager Tommy LaSorda feels. In game one of the 1988 World Series, the Dodgers were behind 4-3 to the Oakland A's, who were heavily favored to win it all.

Taking this first game was essential in almost everyone's eyes. In the bottom of the ninth inning with two outs and a runner on base, LaSorda called on Kirk Gibson to pinch-hit. The leading hitter for LA all season, Gibson was not expected to play in the Series at all. His knees hurt so badly he could hardly walk to the plate. He fouled off the first two pitches. Oakland ace reliever Dennis Eckersley had the look of a matador ready to finish the bull. The pitch arrived at the plate. Whack! Gibson hit a home run to win that game, and the Dodgers won the Series in five. LaSorda looked like a seer for making the substitution.

A local junior high coach found a unique approach to his subbing dilemma. Even though Steve Heck makes certain all of his boys see action each game, one young man became discouraged and was close to quitting because he felt he was getting shorted on playing time. Coach Heck took the problem to the rest of the squad. "What do you think about Travis?" he asked the other players. "Am I being unfair to Travis?" Various players spoke up that they thought Travis was a good kid, that he really tried hard, and deserved more floor time. "Okay, guys, you have to help me out here," said Heck. "Who wants to give up some of **your** playing time?" After a few moments, Brian spoke up, "Coach, I wouldn't mind sitting the bench for a minute or so." "Yeah, me, too," chimed in another player. Even some players who saw limited action themselves were willing to pledge 30 seconds of their time. These young men not only learned a valuable lesson about personal sacrifice, but they became a stronger team for their unselfish actions.

Imagine you were Travis. How would it make you feel to know your teammates thought enough of you to give up some of their own playing time? How much harder must he have cheered for them when he **was** on the bench — and vice versa!

Someone gave up His starring role and was willing to not only sit the bench alongside the rest of humanity, but He made the greatest sacrifice of all time. God, our loving Father, sent Jesus into the game of life as the final substitute for the sins of all mankind. Jesus left His heavenly home to be born in a lowly manger — to face, as a man, the same trials and daily issues that we do. He suffered and died, sacrificing more than we ever could.

What a perfect call God made! What a miracle indeed!

"For God did not send his Son into the world to condemn the world, but to save the world through him" (John 3:17).

"Kirk Gibson never even came out of the clubhouse for introductions, and he never had another at-bat the rest of the World Series. That was the most dramatic home run I've ever seen." — Tommy LaSorda

Lesson 22
Mr. Coach
and Mrs. Athlete

One of the most poignant photos of the 1996 Olympics was that of U.S. heptathlete Jackie Joyner-Kersee as she limped off the track on the arm of her husband-coach, Bobby. He had just informed her she would be withdrawing from the event. She had a pulled hamstring that was so obviously bothering her ability to perform that Bobby felt he had no choice.

"That's enough," he said. "I'm no longer going to allow you to do this. This isn't a coach-and-athlete thing. This is your husband talking. It's time for you to go." One has to wonder who felt worse. It must have been as difficult for him to speak those words as it was for her to hear.

When he pulled Jackie from the heptathlon, he did so in hopes she would heal well enough to compete in the long jump later in the games. She won the bronze medal, her second in four Olympic appearances. She already owned three Olympic gold medals, a silver, and a bronze before coming to Atlanta. A historic figure in track and field since the early eighties, she met Bobby when she set two NCAA records in 1982 and 1983 at UCLA where she was on a basketball scholarship. Bobby coached Jackie in track for the Bruins and they were married in 1986.

Bobby has coached other Olympic athletes including Gail Devers, 1996 Olympic gold medalist in the 100-meter sprint, and Valerie Brisco-

Hooks, who swept the 200 and 400 meters in the 1984 Los Angeles Olympics.

However, coaching Jackie was different. She so out-distanced other female athletes in most of her events that Bobby tried to find new ways to motivate her. He would not let her take his last name until she set the world record in the heptathlon. She broke the record and then re-established her own record four more times — scoring over 7,000 points, a first in women's athletic history. Bobby once bought her two diamond rings for her 30th birthday — one with seven diamonds and one with three. This was his way of encouraging her to aim for 7,300 points in the heptathlon.

Joyner-Kersee also holds the American record in the long jump. She has over 25 prestigious awards in her career, including the Sullivan Award for the best amateur athlete and several Athlete-of-the-Year awards from *The Sporting News* and other groups.

You don't need to hold a record or own a gold medal to need the support of a spouse. In the ordinary ups and downs of life, we can all use someone to lean on for encouragement and motivation. Hopefully, that is something that we can learn to do for one another in our homes.

The major issue that usually causes a crisis is one of control. Who is in control? Egos, dreams, past environment (how we saw our parents react to one another), and peer pressure (reading all those magazine articles) help make for conflict. The authors (Minirth-Newman-Hemfelt) of *Passages of Marriage* offer some healthy suggestions. "Compromise. Everyone gives in a little." Sometimes the compromise may be on who gets to rule on which issue, and often the talents of the two individuals will lend to a natural decision in several areas.

Another key is learning to "agree to disagree." Not every issue has to be a win-lose event. The best is a win-win situation, which might sometimes mean doing your own thing separately. The authors' final suggestion regarding control and conflict is: "Argue over issues, but never allow your conflict to get personal."

"Take your*self* out of it."

"Wives, submit to your husbands as to the Lord. . . . Husbands, love your wives, just as Christ loved the church and gave himself up for her" (Eph. 5: 22–25).

"On the track, he's the CEO and I'm the employee. At home it's husband and wife, and if I don't want to do something, I'm not going to." — Jackie Joyner-Kersee

Lesson 23
Knight Court

Two men head successful NCAA basketball programs. Yet their coaching styles are as different as night and day — make that Knight and "K." As of the 1995–96 season, Bobby Knight had led Indiana to three NCAA titles and was tied as the third winningest coach on the active list (tied for seventh on the all-time list). Mike Krzyzewski (often called Coach "K") had taken Duke teams to six of ten NCAA Final Fours in a ten-year period, winning back-to-back titles in 1992 and 1993. These two men, however, share much more than successful records.

After graduating from Ohio State (playing on the Buckeye 1960 Championship and 1961–62 second place teams), Knight joined the army and was appointed an assistant coach at West Point, and later, head coach.

Krzyzewski played for Knight at West Point. He may have seen Knight's toughness, but he also saw another side to the highly controversial coach. When Krzyzewski's father died, Knight flew to Chicago to join the family in their grief. He wanted to assure his cadet-player that it was fine for him to miss upcoming games to spend time with his family. Krzyzewski elected to return for the tournament. After graduation he then coached for army at their military prep school.

Knight moved on to Indiana and Krzyzewski joined him as an assistant in 1975 before returning to West Point as head coach himself for five years. At Duke University since 1981, Coach "K" still talks affectionately of Knight and his and compassion during the difficult days following his father's death.

Up Close Prime Time host Roy Firestone questioned Knight about why he doesn't let the media know about this kinder side of his personality. "It's no one's business," said Knight. "That's not my story to tell. The story is about Mike and his commitment to the team."

Another Knight devotee is Quinn Buckner. Dejected after being let go from the NBA, he appreciated Knight's vote of confidence when hired as an assistant coach for his alma mater. He also appreciated Knight's recruiting him years earlier as a player. "You want to play for that man because he's honest," Buckner's dad had said. "He won't lie to you. That's a rare com-modity in this world." Knight lived up to this assessment. Says Buckner, "Coach never lied to me."

Honesty is certainly one character quality we should all value. In *The Book of Virtues*, William Bennett reminds us that honesty goes beyond truth-telling. He appreciates parents warning their child when caught in a lie. "Don't let me catch you doing that again!" is fine, but he believes it goes beyond that. Bennett says that moral development is not a game of "catch me if you can." He says honesty is a "disposition to live in the light" — acting "justly" at all times. Do we live in the "light?"

"If we claim to have fellowship with him yet walk in the darkness, we lie and do not live by the truth" (1 John 1:6).

"Coach Knight was a great teacher in terms of basketball, but he was a greater teacher in terms of preparing you for life." — Isaiah Thomas (IU graduate, former Detroit Piston, NBA Hall of Fame, and now vice president of the Toronto Raptors)

Lesson 24
Smooth Sailing

Dennis Conner, captain of victorious America's Cup crews in 1980, 1987, and 1988, grew up as a "wharf rat." His father was a commercial fisherman and his childhood home was two blocks from the San Diego Yacht Club.

Conner became a junior member of the club at age 11. He was assigned as "boat boy" to handle lines, wash the boat, and be a basic errand boy for Bill Buchan. "For me, it was like winning the lottery," says Conner. Buchan was a Seattle boat builder who won several Star World titles and an Olympic gold medal in 1984.

Conner went on to work nearly every role of a crew. He says, "Doing every job — from wet-sanding to working the foredeck to wiggling the tiller — has helped me immeasurably with how I treat my crew and skippering my boat." This overall knowledge of the tasks, plus respect for those who do them well, helped Conner reach the top level of the sport.

Prior to acquiring cable networks (including TNT and CNN) and professional ball teams (Atlanta Braves and Hawks), Ted Turner was an America's Cup yachtsman as well. He skippered the *Mariner* in 1974 and asked Conner to be his number-two man. In addition to the America's Cup victories, Conner won four Southern Ocean Racing Conference titles, two Star Boat World Championships, and an Olympic bronze medal.

Whether racing for trophies or enjoying a leisurely afternoon on a midwestern lake, a basic understanding of how the combination of wind and water surface interact is necessary if you want to sail.

Three factors move a sailboat: the helm (the rudder or an actual wheel in larger boats), the heel (tilt of the boat on its side), and the sails. Conner reminds us, "Sails are the engines of the boat." Using the wind in the sails means learning two basic skills: trimming the sails and tacking.

Trimming is adjusting the sails to take advantage of the available wind. When sailing with the wind (called running), the sail is at a right angle to the direction the boat is heading. While running is relatively easy, it is also the slower way to sail. For more speed or when there is a crosswind, the maneuver is called reaching. This means turning the sail at a lesser angle (for instance, 45 degrees) while tilting the boat slightly on its side. Especially in small boats, sailors need to know how to balance these two maneuvers to avoid capsizing the vessel.

What about sailing directly into the wind? Keeping the sails as parallel to the boat as possible is one maneuver, but you may not go anywhere. This is where tacking comes into play. Tacking is done by changing directions of the sails and making a "Z" movement through the water. With a good wind and smooth water surface, this zigzag needs to be at narrow angles. With either a light wind and/or rougher seas, a wider angle is a safer maneuver.

Moving from a sheltered area like a cove into a brisk wind can easily capsize a boat if you are not prepared. Former chaplain at Christ Hospital in Cincinnati, L.H. Mayfield found himself in this quick-change situation one afternoon. The friend with whom he was sailing shouted, "Let go of the sail!" Mayfield turned the sail loose. As the sail flapped almost out of control, the boat righted itself. He was then able to "pull the sail into the wind" as he gauged "how much the boat could take."

Mayfield was struck with the thought that the very "wind that could have destroyed us was now working for us." We can face other issues in life the same way. We struggle to maintain our own control, perhaps at work or with some family issue. However, when we let go, sometimes admitting our helplessness, then God can take over. With Him in control, our lives will right themselves again.

Even during the storms of life, God can calm our troubled hearts.

"He [Jesus] got up and rebuked the wind and the raging waters; the storm subsided, and all was calm" (Luke 8:24).

"One of my strengths in sailing is that I've worked my way from the bottom of the ladder to the top." — Dennis Conner

Lesson 25
Coaching Your Child

Montreal manager Felipe Alou coached his son Moises with the Expos until the younger Alou left to play for the Florida Marlins. Former Baltimore manager Cal Ripken Sr. coached both of his sons during spring training. Cal Jr. was already a star shortstop when brother Billy played second base in the Oriole minor leagues. Before leaving for Kansas City, Bob Boone had a similar privilege when coaching with Cincinnati. His son Bret was already playing second base for the Reds when younger brother Aaron arrived in the Reds farm system.

Former Miami Dolphin coaching great Don Shula mentored his son Dave who went on to coach the Cincinnati Bengals. *Winning's Only Part of the Game* is a book by and about Florida State football coach Bobby Bowden and his family. His son Terry is head football coach at Auburn while another son Tommy leads the Tulane program.

Arkansas basketball coach Nolan Richardson has Nolan III as an assistant on his bench. A reverse tag-team was seen when head coach Steve Alford hired his dad as an assistant for Southwest Missouri State.

Fathers and sons form special bonds through sports. That is becoming more of a reality for moms and daughters as well with more females breaking into the coaching ranks and higher levels of athletics for women.

Mom or Dad, if you decide to coach your own child, first keep in mind your child's level of interest. Recognized in the Tennis Hall of Fame as one of the game's outstanding coaches, former USTA pro and Davis Cup

Steve Alford
Southwest Missouri State University

member Ron Halmberg warns that we should "expose" our children to the game — "not push!" "RELAX!" says Halmberg. "Young players certainly need direction, but the word is direction, not dominance."

Playing time often becomes a big issue. Other parents may accuse you of favoritism. Don't overreact by benching your own child more than she/he deserves because it's easier than hearing others' complaints. Be careful not to come down excessively on your own child in order to make a point. (Your child may soon decide not to play, when all she/he needs is another coach.)

Don't become the coach "because no one else would volunteer." Unless you really want to do it, the kids will soon sense your "burden" by your attitude.

Ask your child before you commit to the role. Some parents (usually former stars or frustrated players themselves) are chomping at the bit to prove how great they can be. This is your child's time for glory — not yours.

By all means, make it fun! If the activity becomes more argumentative then enjoyable, a change needs to be made. If your child still likes the game, the change needs to be you!

Tom Felton, head of Sports Outreach America, suggests you will need: "Love and concern for the players. Patience and careful planning. Positive reinforcements. Respect for the athletes, opponents, and the game. Fairness and integrity. Not worrying solely about winning, but building character and values." He also reminds us that we (and the team) need balance in our lives.

All of these are the same characteristics we need in everyday parenting. Indeed, we're in the character-building game. Most of us recognize the need to be loving, patient, positive, fair, and honest with our kids. But do we truly respect our children as individuals?

President of Taylor University and the founder of Youth for Christ, Dr. Jay Kesler says that one of the ways we fail as parents is in minimizing our kids' problems. "If a little child has a problem, it's a smaller problem that if an adult has a problem," says Kesler. "In reality, this is not true at all." He reminds us that some of the most critical questions in the world [especially those dealing with character] are asked before the third grade.

Kesler also suggests that our kids need to know we are never too preoccupied with business (even the "Lord's work") to have time for them. This is the best way we can teach children to find balance in their life — by example. Are we surprised?!

"Fathers, don't scold your children so much that they become discouraged and quit trying" (Col. 3:21;TLB).

"I would be jealous sometimes of the relationship that my father seemed to have with some of this players. He may have been a bigger influence in their lives than he was mine, simply because he was with them in a more intense relationship." — Vince Lombardi Jr.

Lesson 26
Elegance and Grace

Fifteen-year-old Michelle Kwan skated a near-perfect program to win the 1996 World Figure Skating Championship. Leading after the short program by only a narrow margin, Kwan had to wait while defending world champion, China's Chen Lu, skated a long program that received two perfect 6.0's. "Chen elegantly threw down the gauntlet with a mesmerizing performance in which she landed six triple jumps, including two in combination," wrote *Sports Illustrated's* E.M. Swift.

Back in the arena's waiting area, Frank Carroll, Kwan's coach, told her to believe in herself and reminded her the judges had left a small window of opportunity. Then she was on the ice. In the midst of these pressure-filled moments, Kwan was amazingly able to remember an option they had discussed in practice in case she had to turn an early triple-triple-combination into only a triple-double jump. When that happened, Kwan threw in an additional triple at the last minute. It may have been what won the world title for her. She had one more triple than Chen and scored two 6.0's of her own plus seven 5.9's.

In her book, *Inside Edge*, Christine Brennen says Kwan and Carroll are "a perfect fit." Brennen sees Carroll so trustworthy, she refers to him as "the Mr. Rogers of figure skating." In addition to skating technique, he coaches Kwan in breathing, smiling, costumes, and even cosmetics. For Kwan to win in women's skating, Carroll felt she needed to remove her child-like image from the judges' minds. He persuaded Kwan and her parents to let her use more make-up. "It's part of the schtick," said Carroll. They also transformed her youthful ponytail into a sophisticated bun with braids tightly coiled with yarn.

However, all the elegant braids, cosmetics, and beaded performance dresses in the universe won't make a skater into a winner. Kwan had also toured with professionals throughout the year which Carroll believed strengthened her skating ability. "Great skating breeds great skating," he said.

Skating at all levels has long been competitive between strength and jumps versus elegance and grace on the ice. Even the graceful Kwan landed six triple jumps in the 1997 World Championships, but still lost to tiny 14-year-old Tara Lipinksi, who landed the first ever triple-loop triple-loop combination in women's figure skating competition. (Lipinksi also replaced Sonja Henie as the youngest skater to win the women's world title.) Canadian Elvis Stojko won the 1997 Men's World Championship with a powerful routine that included a quadruple-triple combination. Perhaps power and athleticism is beginning to garner the attention of the judges.

In previous years, sister and brother Isabelle and Paul Duschesnay captivated audiences with their inventive and athletic dance programs, but the 1992 gold medal was won by the graceful beauty of Marina Klimova and Sergei Ponomarenko. Elegance also took the pairs gold in Albertville with Natalia Mishkutionok and Artur Dmitriev getting all nine judges' first-place ballots. Judges in the 1994 Olympics preferred the romantic elegance of Alexei Urmanov over Elvis Stojko who incorporated a lot of his martial arts training into his performances.

In 1994 gold medalist Oksana Baiul's rendition of "Swan Lake" was one of the most graceful performances of the Olympics. Husband and wife Sergei Grinkov and Ekaterina Gordeeva captured audiences' hearts and judges' votes with their graceful performances to win the pairs gold in both 1988 and 1994. When Grinkov died of a sudden heart attack in 1996, Gordeeva proved she was both graceful and grace-filled. Sharing her grief with fans, Gordeeva is now back on the ice skating solo performances.

Grace also plays a vital role in our Christian lives. Society wants us to believe that we can earn a sense of righteousness through our own power and good deeds. However, true righteousness is a gift of grace. Grace is the very essence of God. It is His unmerited presence and favor in our lives. Grace is the love, acceptance, and forgiveness that each of us long for in our souls that nothing else can fulfill. Christ's forgiveness brings us salvation and a second chance or rebirth. Founder of the Methodist Church, John Wesley said that means of grace are those actions that influence us spiritually and reach into our hearts to connect us to Christ.

"The grace of our Lord was poured out on me abundantly, along with the faith and love that are in Christ Jesus" (1 Tim. 1:14).

"In other sports, you can have a rematch, another golf or tennis tournament, another game next week. But not in this sport. Three and a half minutes and it's over. There's no second chance." — Carol Heiss Jenkins (1960 Olympic gold medalist, married to 1956 gold medalist Hayes Jenkins)

Lesson 27
The Gatorade "Dump"

The Gatorade bath of the winning coach has become the symbol of victory in football today. In one *Sportscenter* segment Bob Ley suggested proper execution: 1. Stay out of the coach's view, even employing another player as a decoy if necessary. 2. Use a high release to get all of the liquid on the coach, making certain there is no contact between the bucket itself and the coach.

NY Giants linebacker Harry Carson ran the first documented "dunk" route on Coach Bill Parcells back in 1986. It is estimated that Parcells has received 73 dunks totaling more than 500 gallons of the popular drink. Once called "kick-a-poo juice" and Cade's Ade (for its inventor), the drink was developed in 1966 as a mineral replacement fluid for the University of Florida football team, whose nickname soon appeared on the label.

With the Cowboys thrashing the Bills (52-17) in Super Bowl XXVII, the most dramatic moment was waiting to see if coach Jimmy Johnson's well-coifed hair would move during the drink dump. His hair survived even another Super Bowl dousing the following year, but Johnson would incur another surprising dump at the hands of Cowboys' owner Jerry Jones. After leading Dallas to four play-offs in five years with two Super Bowl championships, Johnson was replaced by Barry Switzer after the Cowboys lost the 1995 NFC championship game to San Francisco.

Coaching (or managing in baseball) has become a revolving door profession. The door in Cincinnati has ushered out some pretty successful managers. Sparky Anderson led the Big Red Machine of the 1970s to four pennants in seven years with back-to-back World Series championships in '75 and '76. After two seasons in second place, he was fired in 1979. In 1990, Lou Piniella skippered the Reds to the only wire-to-wire season in major league history. They led from opening day, beat the Pirates 4-2 for the pennant, and swept the Athletics in the World Series. Piniella was let go after the next season. (Hired by the Mariners, he would be AL Manager-of-the-Year in 1995.) Davey Johnson led the Reds to first place in their division during the strike-shortened '94 season. The next year the Reds defeated the Dodgers in post-season play before falling to the Braves (the eventual World Series champs). However, Reds' GM Marge Schott had already designated Ray Knight as assistant manager to take over in '96. Johnson moved on to Baltimore taking the Orioles to the 1996 American League championship, losing to the Yankees who won the World Series.

Since basketball coaching icon John Wooden left UCLA in 1975 (with ten NCAA titles), no coach had lasted more than four years until Jim Harrick took over in 1989. Yet they all had winning records: Gene Bartow (1975–77), Gary Cunningham (1977–79), Larry Brown (1979–81), Larry Farmer (1981–84) and Walt Hazzard (1984–88). When Harrick led UCLA to the NCAA championship in 1995, sports broadcaster Dick Vitale claimed Harrick was "the real star of Tinseltown." However, Harrick was let go during the 1996 pre-season when a seemingly minor NCAA rules infraction was thrown at him.

Heralded as a prophet but slaughtered like a lamb — sound familiar?

Having taught and ministered to the people's needs, Jesus was sought after by the crowds. When He rode into Jerusalem on a donkey, throngs of well-wishers had strewn palm leaves and cloaks in His pathway. "Hosanna!" they hailed. "Blessed is he who comes in the name of the Lord!" (Matt. 21:1–11).

Yet in only a few short days, he was arrested, found guilty before Pilate, scourged, mocked, and crucified as His followers first looked on and then ran into hiding. Peter, who had to that moment been the most outspoken, denied even knowing Jesus.

Amazingly, people still deny Him today. He died on Calvary so all people's sins might be forgiven and we might come to a direct and loving relationship with God once again. Christ's blood was "dumped" on our sins so that we might have the real victory!

"In him [Christ Jesus] we have redemption through his blood, the forgiveness of sins, in accordance with the riches of God's grace" (Eph. 1:7).

"I guess what happens in this world is that the Lord will wake you up. He allows things to happen that will get your attention." — Lou Piniella

Lesson 28
Life beyond Death

What causes a man who has already reached the pinnacle in his sport to continue playing a match when he is gut-wrenchingly ill? Ask Pete Sampras. In the quarterfinals of the 1996 U.S. Tennis Open, Sampras was so sick he was throwing up behind the baseline. Playing against Alex Corretja, Sampras persevered for over four hours to win the five-set (including two tie-breakers) match. "This one was for Tim," said Sampras moments after the match, "Tim was there with me."

He was talking about his coach, Tim Gullickson who had died of brain cancer four months earlier. Ranked number one in the world, Sampras didn't need the victory, but he wanted desperately to win a Grand Slam event that year in Tim's memory. Sampras bowed out early in the Australian Open, made it only to the semi-finals of the French Open, and lost in the quarterfinals at Wimbledon. The U.S. Open was his last chance, and fittingly he won it on the very day that would have been Gullickson's 45th birthday.

As a professional tour player, Gullickson ranked as high as #18 in singles (1978) and had won four titles plus 16 doubles titles, 10 of them with his twin, Tom. After retiring in 1986 he turned to coaching. In addition to Sampras, he helped such stars as Martina Navratilova, Aaron Krickstein, and Mary Joe Fernandez. His playing days as well as his coaching technique involved a positive attitude and a zest for life.

When he was struck with brain cancer, he maintained those two philosophies and waged a courageous battle. Along with family and friends, he established the Tim and Tom Gullickson Foundation. Its mission is to assist brain tumor patients and their families in managing not just the physical but emotional and social challenges of the disease.

Sampras served as a pallbearer at Tim's funeral. The story was a reminder of the 1995 Masters. Ben Crenshaw and fellow PGA member Tom Kite were pallbearers at the funeral of longtime mentor and friend Harvey Penick. When Crenshaw won the prestigious tournament, he said he had felt Harvey's spirit during every round.

We never forget the lessons mentors leave with us. North Carolina State basketball coach Jim Valvano is another example. Before succumbing to cancer, Valvano accepted the 1995 ESPY Arthur Ashe Award for Courage. He inspired everyone with his speech that evening. "Do three things each day — think, laugh, and cry." A year later, ESPN *Sportscenter* host Bob Ley spoke in the coach's memory: "Wherever there is a human spirit refusing to give up, Jim Valvano can and always will be found."

We all draw from the memories and spirits of loved ones who precede us in death. Patrick Benson, son of author and speaker Bob Benson, says, "I don't really want to live in memory of Dad, but I do want to live in the hope and the love and the dream that he gave us. We can't recreate what we were, but we can create something new out of what we had."

What are we recreating from memories of loved ones? Of Christ?

"The memory of the righteous will be a blessing" (Prov. 10:7).

"Cancer may take away my physical ability, but it can't touch my heart, my soul, or my spirit." — Jimmy Valvano

Lesson 29
Always Learning More

Dave Chambers not only played on Canada's national hockey team but he has spent over 20 years coaching the sport at nearly every level. He has coached junior college and university athletes and international teams. He was also an assistant and then head coach of the Quebec Nordiques and Minnesota North Stars.

In his book, *Complete Hockey Instruction*, Chambers offers effective coaching techniques that transcend to coaches of all sports. He explains the necessity of having organizational skills, the need for knowledge of training and conditioning methods, and the ability to motivate and "handle" athletes. He also talks about being dedicated, enthusiastic, mature, and fair. Being able to put together a game plan or strategy, evaluate players and other personnel, teach the basics, and effectively run active practices are other responsibilities of a good coach. Communication with the players and the media is also important. Chambers also reminds us that "not all situations in sports are serious." He says to maintain a good sense of humor.

However, the number one thing Chambers believes an effective coach must have is a sound knowledge of his sport and the willingness to read about and observe other methods in order to constantly learn more about the game. He suggests attending clinics as another means of being both a teacher and teachable.

One of the premier golf coaches in PGA history, Harvey Penick also believed it was important to continually learn more about the game he loved and taught. "When people ask who my teacher was, I say — everybody!" he said. "I especially liked listening to teachers (at PGA schools) who taught differently than I do," said Penick. "They made me think."

Many coaches around the nation from various athletic fields attend coaching clinics that help teach motivation and character development far beyond the world of sports. *Athletes in Action* and *Fellowship of Christian Athletes* hold Coaches Camps every year. They also co-sponsored a special Coaches Conference in connection with the 1996 Promise Keepers in Indianapolis. "The most influential adults in the life of an athlete are Mom, Dad, and coach, and with today's family situation, it often becomes Mom and coach," say the conference leaders.

Since they believe coaches are highly influential people, part of their philosophy is to teach these leaders the difference between being a secular athlete and a Christian athlete. The secular view of the world says, "I am the center of the team. My purpose comes from making me look and feel good. God has nothing to do with competition." AIA and FCA suggests that a Christian view is, "God is the center of my world. I want to know and love Jesus Christ. I have been given talents to use to glorify Him and to make Him known."

University of South Carolina head football coach Brad Scott has attended the FCA Coaches Camp. "What a great way to start your season as a coach," he shares, "to be surrounded by Christian coaches and make a recommitment to yourself, your family, and most importantly, to God." Coaches' spouses and families are included in activities at the camps. The Gamecock coach appreciated how the FCA Camp helped him re-prioritize and encouraged him in all areas of his life.

All of us, coaches and non-athletes alike, need time away from our daily routines and chores to think about our priorities and goals in relation to Christ and others. Sign up for a retreat at your church. Look into inter-denominational weekends like the *Walk to Emmaus* (called *Cursillo* in the Catholic Church). Listen to Christian radio for special conferences like *Promise Keepers* (for men) and *Women of Faith — Joyful Journey* (for women). Many local retreat centers also offer one-day (and longer) spiritual growth programs.

Remaining teachable by God's Holy Spirit is one of the most important keys to a successful Christian life. What have you learned lately?

"Instruct a wise man and he will be wiser still; teach a righteous man and he will add to his learning" (Prov. 9:9).

"I felt God had put me in places that gave me training. . . . I'm a firm believer that the Lord has a purpose for everything." — Tony Dungy (Head coach of the Tampa Bay Buccaneers)

Lesson 30
Heart or Head Games

John Hickey (*ESPNET SportsZone*) wrote a series on the managerial styles in major league baseball. "Players' managers" usually relate in more casual and friendly ways with the team, sometimes even asking their opinions. "Managers' managers" take more control and are better known for insight of the game and strategy in making use of the individual abilities of the team. (Hickey included a third type he calls "owners' managers" whose loyalty and decisions are often controlled by the front office.)

Has one coaching method proven more successful? Check recent World Series. Joe Torre, Bobby Cox, and Mike Hargrove are all considered players' managers. Torre led the Yankees to the 1996 Series title. (See the chapter "Dreams Do Come True.")

Cox has mixed veterans and youth in Atlanta into a well-gelled unit. From 1991–1996 the Braves missed only one October Series (in 1993), winning the title in 1995. (This doesn't count the 1994 strike-canceled Series.) Hargrove was Cleveland's manager on the losing end of that 1995 match-up with the Indians. Other managers in the "players'" category are Texas Ranger Johnny Oates (1996 Co-Manager-of-the-Year with Torre) and Montreal Expo Felipe Alou (who has worked near miracles while management continued to trade away the team's major talent.)

The Sporting News 1996 Baseball Yearbook polled a cross-section of executives, managers, coaches, and players to find the top manager in each league. Jim Leyland (still with the Pirates at the time of the survey) and Tony LaRussa (still with Oakland) were the winners.

Leyland came in first in all six categories: in-game strategy, knowledge of the league, handling a pitching staff, motivating players, evaluating young talent, and utilizing available talent. (Like the Expos, the Pirates tend to trade away a lot of top talent.)

Leyland and LaRussa share a unique history. Born only three months apart in 1944, both began their careers in the minors (Southern League) in 1967. When LaRussa coached the White Sox (1982–85), Leyland became his third-base coach. The two remain close friends, but it has been somewhat awkward to talk much baseball (especially strategy) since LaRussa came to the National League (Cardinals) in 1996. (Leyland moved on to the Marlins at the end of the '96 season.)

It didn't take LaRussa long to learn the new league. In his first season, he led St. Louis to the league title round, losing to the Braves in a full seven-game series. LaRussa ranks highest in his game strategy and handling of the pitchers. He says, "What I watch are the other managers."

Other managers classified in LaRussa's and Leyland's style are Baltimore's Davey Johnson (led the Reds to the NL play-offs in 1995 and the Orioles to the AL series in 1996) and Seattle's Lou Piniella (1995 AL Manager-of-the-Year, taking the Mariners to that league series).

While a "manager's manager" rules mostly from his head, the "player's manager" often rules from his heart. Obviously, managers are usually some blend of the two.

In a similar vein, we need to keep a balance in our spiritual walks with

God. We need to love Christ (and others) with both our heads and our hearts.

Some people believe, "Go for the heart. Once you've won the heart, you can train the mind." But sometimes people who find their salvation through emotional pleas and pressure later feel their faith has left them when their feelings are not as intense. We must also have a clear understanding of who Jesus is and what our commitment to Him means.

Michael Vilardo, a United Methodist minister, shares the reason for combining our feelings and intellect. "If our faith is based solely on heart experience, it may be here one minute and gone the next. However, if our faith is based solely on head experience, we will miss out on the passion of a life with Christ as a personal friend."

Won't you give both your heart and head to Jesus?

[Jesus gives us the greatest commandment:] *"Love the Lord your God with all your heart and with all your soul and with all your mind and with all your strength"* (Mark 12:30).

"Jimmy [Leyland] was the one who told me in 1982 that I had to let players see the other side of me, a lighter side, or else they would flame out." — Tony LaRussa

Sources & Recommended Reading

In accordance with copyright laws, all quotations are brief enough in nature and not in competition with any of the following texts and sources that written permission was not necessary. However, we do wish to acknowledge these authors and individuals and encourage you to purchase the books for further reading.

Akers, Michelle. "Never in Her Wildest Dreams...." (Fellowship of Christian Athletes) *Sharing the Victory*, May 1996.

Anderson, Sparky (with Dan Ewald). *Sparky* New York, NY: Prentice Hall Press, 1990.

Athletes in Action, P.O. Box 588, Lebanon, OH 45036. (1-513-933-2421.)

Coaches Ministry: 4001 N.E. Lakewood Way, Lee's Summit, MO 64064. (1-816-795-8242.)

Barcelona—Albertville 1992. The Official Publication of the U.S. Olympic Committee. Salt Lake City, UT: Mikko Laitinen Commemorative Publications, 1992.

Bauer, Gerhard. *Soccer Techniques, Tactics & Teamwork*. New York, NY: Sterling Publishing Co. Inc., 1993.

Bennett, William J. *The Book of Virtues*. New York, NY: Simon & Schuster, 1993.

Benson, Bob. "I Likes To Be Chose," & "The Box Is Too Small," *See You at the House*. Nashville, TN: Generoux, Inc., 1986.

Bentz, Rob. "A New Lou," *Sports Spectrum*, July 1996.

Bohall, Larry D. "Coach G," *Sports Spectrum*, October 1995.

Brennen, Christine. *Inside Edge*. New York, NY: Scribner, 1996.

Brown, Joanie Stearns & Shirley A. Thompson. *Tennis Camps and Clinics*. Princeton, NJ: Petersen's, 1995.

Chambers, Dave. *Complete Hockey Instruction*. Chicago, IL: Contemporary Books, Inc., 1994.

Clairmont, Patsy. "Sportin' a 'TUDE." Colorado Springs, CO: *Focus on the Family*, 1996.

Clinton, Bill. (text of) Inauguration Speech, *Cincinnati Enquirer*, 1/21/97.

"Coaches Who Shaped the Game," America On-line. 1/14/97.

Collins, Bud (and Zander Hollander). *Bud Collins' Modern Encyclopedia of Tennis*. Detroit, MI: Visible Ink Press, 1980.

Conner, Dennis & Michael Levitt. *Sail Like a Champion*. New York, NY: St. Martin's Press, 1992.

Costas, Bob. Segment on Rafer Johnson during NBC broadcast of the Olympics, August 1996.

"Cradle of Coaches," *Miami Redskins 1994-95 Basketball Media Guide*. Miami University, Oxford, OH.

Daughtery, Paul. "Local Gymnasts closer to Olympics," *Cincinnati Enquirer*, 6/6/96.

Diaz, Gwen. "The Long Road Back," (Tony Dungy), *Sports Spectrum*, January 1997.

Diaz, Jaime. "All Eyes on Tiger," *Sports Illustrated Golf Plus*, Preview Issue 1997.

Diaz, Jaime. "The Big BANG," *Sports Illustrated*, 12/23/96.

"Ditka, Saints sign three-year contract," *Cincinnati Enquirer*, 1/29/97.

Dodderidge, John. "From the editor," (FCA) *Sharing the Victory*, December 1995.

ESPNET SportsZone, Starwave Corporation.

       "Tulane to give Bowden offer to coach say sources," 12/10/96

       "Richard 'Digger' Phelps" - bio

"Exhausted Sampras wins in 5 'for Tim'," *Cincinnati Enquirer*, 9/6/96.

Farber, Michael. "Score One for Women," *Sports Illustrated*, 8/12/96.

Fellowship of Christian Athletes, 8701 Leeds Road, Kansas City, MO 64129-1680. (1-800-289-0909).

Felton, Tom. "Hey, Coach!" *Sports Spectrum*, May 1996.

Fenlon, Dick. "These days, Parseghian confronts tougher battle," *South Bend Dispatch*, 9/27/96

Firestone, Roy. *Best of Up Close*. ESPN, 1/2/97.

Firestone, Roy. *Up Close Prime Time*. ESPN, February 1997.

Freeman, Joel A. *God Is Not Fair*. Green Forest, AR: New Leaf Press, Inc., 1994.

God's Treasury of Virtues. Tulsa, OK: Honor Books, Inc., 1995.

Greer, Will. "Reaching New Heights," (FCA Coaches Camp w/ Brad Scott), *Sharing the Victory*, November 1995.

"Heisman Heroes." ESPN, (JCM Productions), 12/13/96.

"Heptathlon — First Lady of Track," *TV Guide*. Radnor, PA: News America Publications, 7/20/96.

Hickey, John. "View from the Top" (series), *ESPNET SportsZone*, February 1997.

Hickok, Ralph. *A Who's Who of Sports Champions*. New York, NY: Houghton Mifflin Company, 1995.

Hoard, Stephen H. "Even If Our Gospel Is Veiled." Sermon: Trinity United Methodist Church, 2/9/97.

Hollander, Zander. *Inside Sports Hockey*. Detroit, MI: Visible Ink Press, 1997.

"Jackie Joyner-Kersee: The Greatest Ever." PRODIGY Web Browser, www.nbc.com/features, 1996.

Johnson, Michael. *Slaying the Dragon*. New York, NY: Harper Collins Publishers, 1996.

Kesler, Jay. *Family Forum*. Wheaton, IL: Victor Books, 1984.

King, Peter. "Bitter Pill," *Sports Illustrated*, 5/27/96.

King, Peter. "Warmed Up," *Sports Illustrated*, 1/27/97

Lee, Victor. "Felipe Alou: The Expos' Great Catch," *Sports Spectrum*, May 1996.

Ley, Bob. *Sportscenter*, ESPN, 1/14/97.

Ley, Bob. "Titletown, USA," *Outside the Lines*. ESPN, 1/3/97.

Masher, Bill. *Politically Incorrect Calendar*. Comedy Channel, 1996.

"Manager's Biography." *Major League@bat*, America-on-line, 1996.

Marantz, Steve. "Deans of the Dugout," *The Sporting News Baseball Yearbook*, 1996.

Martzke, Rudy. "Summing up the best, worst announcers," *USA Today/Cincinnati Enquirer*, 1/5/97.

Mayfield, L.H. *Behind the Clouds — Light Meditations for Tough Times*. Cincinnati, OH: Wesley Hall, 1991.

Minirth, Frank & Mary Alice, Dr. Brian & Deborah Newman, & Dr. Robert & Susan Hemfelt. *Passages of Marriage*. Nashville, TN: Thomas Nelson Publishers, 1991.

Moore, Kenny. "Coming on Strong," *Sports Illustrated,* 8/5/96.

Myers, Chris. *Up Close*. ESPN, September 1996.

Nack, William. "Answered Prayer," *Sports Illustrated*, 10/14/96.

Neff, Beers, Barton, Taylor, Veerman & Galvin, editors. *Practical Christianity*. Wheaton, IL: Tyndale House Publishers, Inc., 1987.

> Fernando, Ajith. "Does God Speak through the Bible?"
> Foster, Richard. "An Introduction to Spiritual Disciplines."
> Seamands, David. "Forgiveness: The Cure for Resentment."

Nelson, Judith. "Wow! This Is Mine!" *Sports Spectrum*, November 1996.

"1996 Promise Keepers Coaches Conference," hosted by Athletes in Action & Fellowship of Christian Athletes, 1996.

"Nolan Richardson." PRODIGY Web Browser, http:/cavern.uark.edu/hogs/basketball, 1996.

Ogilvie, Lloyd John. *Silent Strength for My Life*. Eugene, OR: Harvest House Publishers, 1990.

Penick, Harvey (with Bud Shrake). *If You Play Golf, You're My Friend*. New York, NY: Simon & Schuster, 1993.

Penick, Harvey (with Bud Shrake). *For All Who Love the Game*. New York, NY: Simon & Schuster, 1995.

Price, S.L. "About Time," (Tony Dungy), *Sports Illustrated*, 6/10/96.

Promise Keepers. P.O. Box 103001, Denver, CO 80250-3001. 1-800-888-7595.

Reds Report, Columbus, OH: Columbus Sports Publications, December 1996 & January 1997.

"Robinson: Give me 1 more year," (The Associated Press), *The Cincinnati Enquirer*, 12/11/96.

Rosaforte, Tim. *Tiger Woods*. New York, NY: St. Martin's Press, 1997.

Rushin, Steve. "A Real Kick," *Sports Illustrated*, 9/16/96.

Shaughnessy, Dan. *Seeing Red — the Red Auerbach Story*. Holbrook, MA: Adams Publishing, 1994.

Shaw, Fred. Sermon: Trinity United Methodist Church, 5/19/96.

Shealy, Dan & Pat Springle. *Accept the Challenge Cuz There's Only ONE WAY TO PLAY!* Nashville, TN: Thomas Nelson Publishers, 1995

Shula, Don & Ken Blanchard. *Everyone's A Coach*. Grand Rapids, MI: Zondervan Publishing, 1995.

Sorrell, Bill. "Our Source of STRENGTH," (FCA) *Sharing the Victory*, February 1996.

Sports Illustrated online, articles about Joe Gibbs, John Madden, Mike Ditka, 1997.

Sports Illustrated 1997 Sports Almanac. New York City, NY: Bishop Books, 1997.

"Sports psychologists help track athletes, coaches," The Associated Press, *Cool Sports*, America-Online, 1996.

Stoughton, Greg. "Elite athlete offers hope through personal memoirs," *Athletes in Action*, Winter 1997.

Stoughton, Greg, *Fourth & One with Joe Gibbs*. (video and training guide produced by Athletes in Action), Orlando, FL: New Life Publications, 1996.

Sullivan, Tim. "Merry-go-round points Tracy toward Atlanta," *The Cincinnati Enquirer,* 6/29/96.

Sullivan, Tim. "Wyche, out of the loop, wants back in," *The Cincinnati Enquirer,* 2/6/97.

"SUMMIT: Ex-president lead volunteers," *The Cincinnati Enquirer,* 2/17/97.

Swindoll, Charles R. *Strengthening Your Grip*. Waco, TX: Word Books, 1982.

Swift, E.M. "Driving Dominique," *Sports Illustrated,* 7/22/96.

Swift, E.M. "Red Hot," *Sports Illustrated,* 4/1/96.

Tim & Tom Gullickson Foundation, 8000 Sears Tower, Chicago, IL, 60606. (312/876-7565).

The "V" Foundation, 1201 Walnut Street, 2nd Floor, Cary, NC 27511. (1-800-4-JIMMY)

Verducci, Tom. "Brave New World," *Sports Illustrated,* 7/15/96.

Verducci, Tom. "A New High," *Sports Illustrated,* 5/27/96.

Verducci, Tom. "Regular Joe," *Sports Illustrated,* 10/26/96.

Verducci, Tom. "Stroke of Fate," *Sports Illustrated,* 11/4/96.

Vilardo, Michael. Sermon: Trinity United Methodist Church, January 1995.

Vitale, Dick (with Dick Weiss). *Holding Court*. Indianapolis, IN: Masters Press (Howard K. Sams & Co.), 1995.

The Walk to Emmaus. (Talks: Means of Grace, Piety, Perseverance). Nashville, TN: The Upper Room, July 1990.

Wolff, Alexander. "Simply the Best," See: *Sports Illustrated 1997 Almanac*.

Women of Faith, (The Joyful Journey). 590 Glenneyre, Suite 107, Laguna Beach, CA 92651. Phone 1-800-266-5745.

Wooden, John (with Jack Tobin). *They Call Me Coach*. Chicago, IL: Contemporary Books, 1980.

"woodenclassic.com." (America on-line), Atheron Communications, 1996.

The World Book Encyclopedia, Volumes 13-M & 17-S/SN. Chicago, IL: World Book, Inc., 1983.

Wuerffel, Danny. "The Sacrifice of Prayer," *Sharing the Victory*, January 1997.

"Yanks' Torre, Rangers' Oates Share AL Manager of Year," *SportsLine USA*, 11/7/96.